LEGAL
— and —
ETHICAL
ISSUES
for
MENTAL HEALTH CLINICIANS

Best Practices for Avoiding Litigation, Complaints and Malpractice

Susan J. Lewis, PhD, JD

Copyright © 2016 by Susan Lewis, PhD, JD

Published by
PESI Publishing & Media
PESI, Inc
3839 White Ave
Eau Claire, WI 54703

Cover: Matt Pabich
Editing: Bookmasters
Layout: Bookmasters and Amy Rubenzer

ISBN: 9781683730125

Printed in the United States of America.

PESI
Publishing
& Media
www.pesipublishing.com

PREFACE

When PESI asked me to write this book, I was overwhelmed. But, I was ignited by the richness of research and my own curiosity. Deep inside I am both a teacher and learner. It has also been my privilege throughout my life to practice clinical and forensic psychology. I entered Boston University School of Law later in my life. Law has allowed me to practice forensic psychology in prisons, courts and forensic hospitals. The law has guided my abilities to give expert testimony and lessen sweating. It has also been an honor to teach in university settings, to students, supervisees and colleagues. PESI has enabled me to teach for many years across the United States, which has allowed me to combine law and ethics in the context of the mental health field with a diversity of people.

I am indebted to my colleagues who attended my lectures on this topic and gave me feedback and suggestions. Their wisdom has guided the content of this book.

Linda Jackson, from PESI, served as my cheerleader throughout this project. She was always supportive and complementary of my work whether it deserved it or not.

Cynthia Dibble encouraged me to write although I would rather have watched television. She ensured that I ate, took my dogs for a walk and made certain I saved my work in the event of a computer catastrophe!

My parents treated education as a priority, which encouraged my travels through lifelong learning. I am indebted to them for exposing me to many different avenues for education.

It is my sincere hope that this book will add to your knowledge and critical thinking, and that my sense of humor sprinkled throughout will make you chuckle.

TABLE OF CONTENTS

CHAPTER 1

RISK MANAGEMENT

Why write a book about law and ethics? Those of us who have entered the field of mental health, in whatever capacity, usually hold the highest levels of integrity and ethics. Why else would anyone enter a helping profession?

Have you ever been in a situation where a client has become enraged with you and threatens to file a malpractice action or a licensing complaint against you? Or, have you made a mistake or done something wrong and you worry that when discovered it will precipitate similar actions? There are hundreds of scenarios that are similarly frightening.

As a budding clinician in graduate school and my internships, I was essentially taught to be a loving, caring, warm human being and capable therapist. The legal system was not touched upon as an important subject matter. My job was to marry my clients and be loyal to them. It was of no concern for me whether they got better or worse, gained insight or not, or benefitted. This was marriage without the option of divorce.

I was lied to.

Society has become far more litigious than ever before. If an individual believes he or she has been harmed, whether inadvertently or with intention, that individual often seeks solutions through legal channels.

Any of us can be sued for anything at any time.

This doesn't mean that all suits will end up in a court of law. Some will be deemed frivolous and proceed no further. Others may not be lucrative enough to beckon the legal profession to take on the challenge. Some will require legal counsel, which is anxiety producing and possibly costly.

Some organizations assure their employees that they will be covered by malpractice policies the agency, hospital, etc., maintains. No need to have your own individual liability insurance. What a generous offer!

However, be crystal clear that each organization is interested in its own viability and the minimization of risk. The organization does not retain its lawyers to ensure adequate representation of its constituency. Simply stated, you will be thrown under a bus alone.

In my thirty years in the field of psychology I have witnessed colleagues who have been sued or had licensing complaints filed against them. Before

> ***Always maintain your own malpractice***
> ***coverage and read the fine print.***

the case reaches resolution, these individuals have lost their source of income, their self-confidence in their expertise, and the reliance on years of education as a foundation for their work. It is career changing and hard to recover from. The penalties imposed by state boards can be costly, lengthy and burdensome. Henceforth, any application for relicensure, which will ask you about board complaints or legal suits, will need to be answered with a yes. Movement from state to state is curtailed because each state will ask the same question. Individual malpractice insurance will increase in price dramatically—you have been branded. A malpractice finding against you could be costly not only in legal fees but remuneration for damages.

> ***Risk management is essential.***
> ***Practicing proactively is part of this strategy.***

As I previously stated, we can all be sued for anything, but it is better to protect ourselves in advance as best we can. This book is about protection. I will present case studies, relevant examples, and talk about what questions we may be asked if we are called to the stand for courtroom testimony. I hope that some of the examples will bring peace of mind as there are preventative steps one can take to minimize the risk of being sued.

The information is not designed to frighten you but to help you be cognizant of pitfalls, and also offer tips to minimize the risk of such occurrences. My goal is for participants to leave my workshops feelings less anxious and more equipped to address the risks of practice.

We are supervisors as well as clinicians. When we train students, I believe we all have the intention of helping each one learn and step into his or her new professional roles. These new students practice under our licenses.

Supervision is a very high-risk endeavor. Let me start with a sobering example.

Case Example

• • • • • • • • • • •

A student was under the tutelage of a licensed clinician for twelve months of a training internship. Twice a week they met for an hour and discussed the content of the conversations the student was having with his clients. The supervisor's methodology required that the supervisee take notes during the session with clients as well as record in-progress notes and summaries of each meeting. Supervisor and supervisee also devoted time to psychodiagnostic assessment and constantly reviewing the course of treatment chosen.

One of a supervisor's tasks is to review the client record each week to make certain the student complies with the guidelines. Not uncharacteristically, this supervisor was working with five students simultaneously. As you can well imagine this produced mounds of paperwork. The supervisor had to cosign each written page by each student.

The reading of each word in every record is laborious. In addition, in order to protect the confidentiality of each client, the record must remain in the record room, meaning many late evenings.

Rather than review each note, the supervisor decided to select arbitrary pages to review and flipped through the remaining ones, signing each one as well. Some pages were signed sight unseen which is not a prudent practice.

The supervisor was concerned about one of the male students he was working with. He decided to meet with that student more often. His concerns were heightened when he learned from the administrative staff that meetings between this student and one specific client were lasting longer than usual. Often when staff tried to find the student for his next patient, they could not find him.

The senior administrative assistant had witnessed the student walking out of the clinic with this client on several occasions. He then had not returned for hours.

When the student was confronted with his unusual behaviors he became defensive. "What is wrong with walking the client out?" he asked.

The supervisor recommended some reading on the nature of boundaries with clients and intended to discuss the topic in supervision.

The student subsequently missed several appointments with his supervisor due to an unexplained illness. Upon his return he told the supervisor that his client had abruptly quit coming to sessions and wouldn't return his phone calls. Together they analyzed the case, trying to figure out what had led to the abrupt termination and different ways the student might have intervened earlier.

Several months later, the supervisor was notified that the clinic as well as the student had been named in a malpractice action brought by the client. The malpractice suit claimed that the supervisor's student had been having an ongoing sexual relationship with the client.

During a confrontation with the student, he admitted to the nature of the relationship. The supervisor had no previous knowledge of an inappropriate relationship. His student had lied to him.

The clinic filed a complaint against the supervisor with the licensing board.

The board's investigation was slow and exacting, leaving the supervisor in limbo. The board's findings were against him and punitive action was taken.

The supervisor was devastated by the board's findings. The licensing board ordered him to be supervised once a week for five years at his own expense, if he wanted to continue in the field. His liability carrier had refused to defend him because in the small print, the contract clearly stated that protective coverage does not cover sex with a patient. He was financially ruined.

The final straw in this saga was that he was unable to find malpractice insurance to protect himself in the future. He gave up his vocation.

He had neglected risk management strategies. Later in this book we will discuss some specific guidelines that supervisors can use to protect themselves in their vulnerable roles.

In addition to risks faced by supervisors, there are also risks faced by those engaged in research. This topic will be discussed in the following section, including a series of research experiments in which proper protections were not offered to the participants.

Psychological Research Sets Standards

In 1961 the famous Stanley Milgram obedience experiment was conducted at Yale University following Adolf Eichmann's trial as a war criminal. The focus of the experiment was on researching how far people would go in obeying an instruction even if it involved harming another person. Eichmann's defense was that he was just following orders from his superiors.

Each participant was paired with another person. One was designated as the "learner" and the other the "teacher." The draw was fixed so the learner was one of Milgram's confederates (pretending to be a real participant).

The "learner" was strapped to a chair with electrodes. After he learned a list of word pairs given to him by the teacher, the teacher would test him by naming a word and asking the learner to recall it from a list of four possible choices.

The teacher was told to administer an electric shock each time the learner made a mistake, increasing the level of shock each time. There were 30 switches on the shock generator marked from 15 volts (slight shock) to 450 (danger—severe shock).

The learner gave mainly wrong answers (on purpose), and for each of these the teacher appeared to give him an electric shock. What the teacher was unaware of was that the learners did not actually receive a shock but simulated pain in response to the shock. When the teacher refused to administer a shock, the experimenter gave a series of orders to ensure the teacher continued.

The results indicated that approximately three-quarters of participants (teachers) continued to the highest level of 450 volts. All the participants continued to 300 volts.

His findings suggested that ordinary people are likely to follow orders given by an authority figure, even to the extent of killing an innocent human being.

There was no internal review board and no demonstrated concern for the effects on the participants.

Dr. Philip Zimbardo conducted a famous experiment in 1971 referred to as the Stanford Prison Experiment. Zimbardo was interested in finding out the roles people play in prisoner situations. He designed the psychological study to try and understand how ordinary people, in this case college students, can behave in aggressive and dehumanizing ways based on a situation. Subjects were divided into two groups, "guards" and "prisoners"; the guards were allowed to inflict escalating levels of pain and humiliation on the prisoners over an extended period of time, which resulted in extreme psychological stress. For six days, half the study's college students endured cruel and dehumanizing abuse by their peers. They were taunted, stripped naked, sleep deprived, humiliated, and forced to use plastic buckets for human waste. Some participants became violent; others withdrew into despair. As the situation increased in intensity, the primary researchers stood by and essentially watched. A colleague spoke up and the experiment was halted.

Between 1963 and 1966 the Willowbrook Hepatitis Study was conducted on mentally retarded institutionalized children. Parents were essentially pressured into consenting to having their children systematically infected with hepatitis.

The US Public Health Service conducted the Tuskegee Syphilis Study between 1932 and 1972. At the time penicillin was the accepted treatment for syphilis. Four hundred rural southern African American men who suffered from the disease were arbitrarily denied treatment.

Why would practitioners enter a helping vocation if they were not ethical, law-abiding, or moral professionals?

Our history leaves a less than honorable story of abuse of vulnerable populations in the name of treatment and research.

What are the ethical standards in our field and how is it different from morality and the laws?

Professional ethics can be understood as a set of guidelines outlining what professionals should or should not do in their profession. The intent is to provide standards of professional conduct. The code of ethics also enhances the profession and keeps the welfare of the people we treat at the forefront of the goals.

The overriding objectives are respect for the rights and dignity of a person, competence, responsibility, and integrity as well as beneficence and non-maleficence (avoidance of harm).

What is the differentiation among law, morality, and ethical considerations?

Law is a system of rules enforced through social institutions to govern behaviors. There are a number of vehicles through which laws can be made. Laws can be made by legislatures resulting in statutes or through the executive by decrees and regulation or by judges through binding precedent, in common law jurisdictions.

Morality may be described as a code of conduct put forward by a society, religion, or accepted by an individual(s) for his or her own behavior. It might be viewed as a system that is to be applied to all people.

As mental health practitioners we are required to not only follow the laws but also the *ethical* guidelines promulgated by each profession.

CRITICAL THINKING

Practitioners are routinely placed in clinical situations where the accuracy of their decisions may be lifesaving as in a suicide risk assessment. What variables might we consider in our decision making?

Case Example

What would you do and what factors might you consider in the following example?

You are a child protective worker investigating a report of suspected medical neglect in a Native American family on a reservation in New Mexico. A report has been made to your agency by one of the medical clinic doctors that a 12-year-old girl may be suffering from life-threatening asthma. The young girl is being denied Western medical treatment. The tribe elder has been treating her with herbal remedies and faith-based prayers. The question to answer is whether the risk to the girl's health is significant enough and warrants the removal of the child from the home, placement in foster care, and medical care to ensure recovery.

Morally, I might feel like putting a saddle on my white stallion that will accommodate two people, prance right into the house where the child resides, swoop the child onto the back of my saddle, and ride into the sunset.

What variables should I consider in making my decision?

a The Law

What are the laws in your state that govern the responsibility to protect children who may be vulnerable or potentially be in physical danger? What are the exact words that are used for your assessment? What are the legal grounds for removal? What kind of data must be presented and to whom? The law, though, is not the only precept to consider.

b Ethical Standards: The Rights of Families to Choose Their Own Medical Care

This subject has been mired in controversy more recently. For example, a religious group, the Jehovah Witnesses, prohibits ingesting blood and accepting blood transfusions. What are the standards of law that set the bar for children who are either seriously ill or in life-threatening circumstances? Do herbal remedies meet those standards?

There have been several recent cases highlighting this question such as parents (or teens) declining chemotherapy, a child in Wisconsin who died of a diabetic coma because her parents prayed for her instead of calling a doctor, and also a case of an autistic child (also in Wisconsin) whose mother took him to a prayer service (where they promised to exorcise the demons from his body), but sadly ended up fatally suffocating the child during the process.

c Cultural and Regional Standards: The Acceptability of Alternative Medical Treatment

d Your Own Professional Standards and Your Views About the Treatment of Children

Recently in the news the controversy of parents declining to vaccinate their children due to fears of a link to autism has been at the forefront.

The decision you are forced to make may not be consonant with your own moral belief system. How do you reconcile your own personal views with decision making in your client's best interest?

Case Example

• • • • • • • • • • •

Your private practice therapy office is near a college campus. You have a contract with the university's counseling center to treat students whom they refer to you. They send a young man to meet with you who has never received any mental health treatment before but his symptoms suggest he may be suffering from depression.

Jerry is in his first semester of his final year of college. He has been a good student, but suddenly he finds his grades are dropping. He reports that he can't concentrate on studying or pay attention in class. He is far behind in his work with exams creeping up.

He has not been sleeping well and finds himself wide awake in the early morning hours and can't fall back asleep. He then feels so tired that he can't get out of his bed in the morning and sometimes spends the day napping. He reports he has lost his appetite and has experienced a dramatic weight loss recently in a short period of time.

Jerry's college career has been spent the way most students experience college life. He has been having sex with many partners, he has a wide circle of friends whom he parties with, and he drinks excessive amounts of alcohol whenever the opportunity presents itself. If there is time left over, he attempts to shift his focus to his schoolwork. He tells you that his concentration is so poor that it takes him three times as long to do his schoolwork.

He is isolating himself from friends, has no motivation, and doesn't feel like he has enough energy to step out of the hole he has found himself in.

"I just feel down, like my world is moving in slow motion and not forward," he says. He continues, "I feel hopeless, I have no energy, and I don't care about anything. There is nothing in my life that sparks my interest. I feel like there is a dark cloud hovering over my head."

Jerry also complains he doesn't feel physically well; his glands are swollen and hurt, he has a sore throat and gets recurrent headaches.

Jerry is a biomedical engineering major and hopes to find employment in one of the large pharmaceutical companies. This first semester of his senior year is crucial in relation to future opportunities. His chosen field is competitive.

During the first semester of his final year of college, recruiters visit different university campuses testing the waters for potential candidates they want to consider for future employment following graduation. Final first semester grades are important because the recruiters strongly weigh them as one of the important criteria.

Jerry reports that he missed a scheduled interview by oversleeping. During another appointment he forgot the content of the conversation. When the interviewer asked him a question, there was an uncomfortable silence as he tried to remember the topic of conversation.

This would be Jerry's first professional venture into the workforce. As the interviews continue Jerry feels he has "not made the cut," which results in his feeling overwhelmed and helpless. As the semester continues and he has received little contact from the recruiters, he is more and more panicked.

Jerry is engaged to be married and has sought the support of his fiancée but feels she is not able to help him. He is desperate, frantic, and frightened. For him the stakes are very high and he believes his performance was below the level at which he usually performs. The result will lessen his options dramatically.

What is your general plan of action to assist this young 19-year-old man? Is there any further information you need to get to develop a course of treatment?

Questions to Consider in Forming a Plan of Action

- What is the legal age of majority in your state? Is Jerry considered an adult? Even though most states designate 18 as the age of majority some states have different laws. For example: In Alabama the age is 19, and in Mississippi it is 21.

- Where is this information? It can be found in the statutes of that state. For example, in Alabama the statute would be designated as Ala Code § 26-1-1: Alabama Code—Section 26-1-1: Age of Majority Designated as 19 Years. Most of this information is readily available on the Internet.

- What are the laws around confidentiality for an adult? Should you call his parents to express your concern and solicit their support? Without a full consent to the release of information from him, the laws of confidentiality bind you.

  A new law was passed recently in Illinois requiring all colleges to provide incoming students with a form allowing them to designate someone who should be called in the case of an emergency. College mental health staff are now required to contact them in case of imminent risk. All providers working in colleges should be encouraged to check if there are specific state laws addressing confidentiality in college settings.

- The somatic complaints necessitate a referral to a physician for a physical examination. It is important that you get a two-way release to communicate with the doctor and the doctor can communicate information in return. What if Jerry refuses?

- What are you considering to be a preliminary working diagnosis? Perhaps depression. Since it is very early in treatment, the extent and severity of the depression is not yet known.

  Given a suspicion of depression, it is important to assess for both suicide risk as well as a level of alcohol/substance use.

- Practice guidelines provide evidence-based recommendations for the assessment and treatment of what appears to be a depressive disorder. You must know what they are. What is the information you need to elicit from your patient?

Evaluation

1. Establishing a therapeutic alliance

2. Evaluation of suicide safety evaluation including level of, so it is level of risk, level of self-care, and risk or harm to self and others

3. Need for psychiatric hospitalization

4. History of substance use

5. Education for the patient about the nature of the illness

6. Assess supports and protective factors

Treatment

1. Medical examination and subsequent contact with the physician

2. Psychiatric assessment and possible referral for medicine

3. Psychotherapy: What is acceptable as the standard of care?
   - Cognitive-behavioral therapy
   - Psychodynamic therapy
   - Problem-solving therapy
   - Combination of medications and psychotherapy

4. Complementary and alternative therapies
   - St. John's wort
   - Acupuncture
   - Exercise

5. Identify a support system

6. Provide off hours coverage options

7. Consider more intensive treatment until crisis period resolves

If you are called into court because a malpractice action (we will discuss the elements of a malpractice action later in the book) has been initiated against you and you have used some other less acceptable modality, you must be prepared to defend yourself.

Jerry consents for you to talk with his university doctor. The news you receive is surprising and troubling. The doctor tells you Jerry is HIV positive.

In addition, the doctor reports that Jerry's blood work has indicated his viral loading is high at this point.

- Is there a duty to warn anyone? What are the laws around duty to warn in your state? Are there specific laws concerning HIV status? Keep in mind that being HIV positive is no longer a death sentence but rather a chronic condition.

  Keep in mind states vary on this topic. Some permit warning, some prohibit warning and a few mandate warning. Consider, however, whether it may be outside of the boundaries of competence to warn based on a medical diagnosis. For example, Illinois forbids warning by mental health professionals.

- If so, who do you warn and what information are you at liberty to share?

The decision-making variables we need to pay attention to are complicated. The requirements of our breadth of knowledge, from both a legal and ethical perspective, has widened substantially in the twenty-first century.

Our society has become far more litigious, seeking settlement using the courts. Hopefully, one of the reasons is because the patients we work with, in whichever setting, have become more sophisticated and expect a higher level of competence. The bar of knowledge we need is higher than it has ever been.

Given the possibility of litigation, it makes sense to practice proactively and defensively thinking in advance of potential scenarios. Given our vulnerability in our work, a risk analysis might be prudent.

There are essentially two ways of practicing in any mental health setting: technological and adaptive.

A technological approach is determined by solid rules. For example, if a clinician has a policy to never make any physical contact with a client (including handshakes) that would be a technological approach applied across all situations. A rule-based approach alleviates uncertainty. It is useful for individuals who are risk aversive.

The American Red Cross's management of unexpected disasters demonstrates a dramatic example. Strategizing for weeks on end would delay rescue efforts. The organization follows a protocol that allows for immediate intervention providing help for those injured.

The adaptive approach provides more latitude in decision making. These decisions would be situationally specific in nature. For example, how do we achieve a work-life balance? The answer depends on many factors and may be applicable solely to a single situation.

Case Example

* * * * * * * * * * * *

You are referred a patient whose life is severely compromised. She has been plagued by forcing herself to redo her taxes weekly for fear of a mistake. When she believes the task is completed, the final step is to submit and resubmit it to the Internal Revenue Service. Rather than relying simply on mail delivery, at the end of each week she telephones the office to make certain it has arrived. As we can well imagine her repeated phone calls are ignored. The cycle then resumes.

In addition, she feels compelled to wash her hands after she has written anything. These compulsions drive her life. She is unable to work since the tasks she has set before herself are laborious and time consuming. She cannot maintain friendships for similar reasons and also because of her embarrassment. Her life is empty and isolated and she reaches out to you in desperation.

Questions to Consider in Forming a Plan of Action

After obtaining an extensive history, what would you consider as a preliminary working diagnosis?

- I would suggest obsessive-compulsive disorder (OCD).

What are practice guidelines based on evidence-based recommendations for the assessment and treatment of OCD?

- The evidence suggests that the standard of care for the effective treatment for OCD is cognitive-behavioral therapy (CBT).
- The strongest evidence supporting CBT is treatment called exposure and response prevention (ERP).

Should you refer the patient to a physician or nurse practitioner who has prescription privileges?

You inform your patient of the treatment plan and assure her of your training in this modality of treatment. In addition, you document your thinking in the progress notes and proceed.

After working with her for six months, she arrives for her appointment one afternoon and explains to you that you have not been helpful to her. She has not felt a decrease in either her anxiety or the need for the repetitive nature of her behaviors.

You have a dilemma. Knowing the standard of care and the strong evidentiary guidelines, what are your options?

You could make a referral to another professional whom you believe has a higher level of expertise. However, your client has already informed you that so far this treatment method has not been effective in helping her change her thinking or behaviors.

When you explore with her what she thinks might be more helpful, she replies that she has not told anyone of her struggles because she is embarrassed. She would like to honestly express her disappointment in how her life is going and the limitations that are self-imposed.

If you elect to change the modality and continue to work with her, you are deviating from the accepted standard of care.

I would suggest that your progress notes reflect your understanding of the accepted standard of care. Explain your reasoning and include what your client has asked for. You are then offered some protection in a court of law if she initiates any legal action. This would be an example of proactive thinking. The intent is to protect yourself yet meet the needs of your client.

CORNERSTONES OF ETHICAL PRACTICE

As clinicians we are tasked with maintaining our skill-based competencies.

How do we do that?
- Training and supervision
- Continuing education
- Consultation
- Keeping up to date with the literature in your specialty
- Professional experience with different populations
- Understanding the marriage between science and evidence-based practice

Clients who want to know about our training and experience have a right to this information. It is important to be honest. Clinicians have at times represented themselves noncommittally. "I use an eclectic approach." You must have the required training for how you professionally present yourself to perspective clients.

What is a specialty?
- Special pursuit, occupational training, aptitude, and skill set

What is proficiency?
- Training in a particular art, occupation, or branch of knowledge

A client believes he is not improving and files legal action against you. You have presented yourself as a specialist in the modality you have used. In courtroom testimony you will need to present your credentials and training to support your areas of specialty.

A simpler analogy: I wouldn't want a dermatologist who took a three-day seminar in open-heart surgery to perform that surgery on me.

FAILURES OF COMPETENCY

- Limited training with certain populations: An area receiving a lot of attention recently is training in working with diverse populations. A clinician may have sufficient training in a technique but not be knowledgeable about its application with a particular population.
- Inaccurate risk assessment: Someone was at a higher risk of suicide than your assessment indicated and a serious though not lethal attempt has been made
- Overextension of one's expertise and confusing one's roles
- Technology used inappropriately

Case Example

You are working with a person for a lengthy time. Initially, when he came to you he expressed whatever he thought. His inability to filter his thoughts from expression had been costly to him in terms of success. He has had difficulty maintaining jobs because he tells his bosses what they are doing wrong without censorship and has the same difficulty maintaining close relationships for the same reasons.

After intensive work the two of you were engaged in, he began to understand the impact of his unedited comments. His life improved as he developed a new skill set. He screened his comments. What he said to others was not hurtful. He gained employment that he was able to maintain and began to be involved with a social network.

During one meeting he tells you that his work has relocated him to another state. He feels frantic and would like to continue his sessions with Skype or Facetime. He intends for you to continue to bill his new insurance carrier. I am certainly pleased when I am successful in helping people improve their lives. It might be tempting.

Most insurance companies require face-to-face contact. Additionally, a practitioner must be licensed in the state in which they are practicing. It is easy to fall into the trap of practicing outside the standard of ethical and legal rules.

Case Example

. . . .

Dr. Ober is a renowned child psychologist with more than twenty-five years of experience doing family and child work, custody and guardian evaluations, and couples mediation. He is a trained mediator having served often in this role for the courts.

He would like to expand his practice and become an expert for the court in his specialty and gain more experience testifying in the courtroom. In this new role the court assigns a case to him. His task is to evaluate a young divorcing couple that has a 6-year-old son and make recommendations to the court addressing any unresolved conflicts.

The couple comes in for their appointment without their young son. Dr. Ober is initially struck by the conciliatory nature in which they communicate with each other. In fact, they have worked out joint legal custody and living arrangements, financial responsibilities, and which parent will transport their son to which sports event and remain for the game.

Dr. Ober is confused as to why the court has ordered the evaluation since it appears all the pertinent issues have been resolved amicably. He asks a series of questions to further assess areas of potential conflict. There doesn't seem to be any unresolved areas of conflict. He reports to the couple his findings and explains what he will be testifying to in court.

He then offers the couple the opportunity to use the process of mediation if there are any remaining incongruities. They agree. Before he proceeds he informs them that information spoken about during mediation will be held in the strictest of confidentiality.

The couple begins to argue with each other about dating others and strangers staying in the household when their son is present. What ensues is more arguing about how flexible childcare is, how much notice needs to be communicated for extra care.

Given the nature of the conversation Dr. Ober suggests that they return to the court evaluation and perhaps come to a compromise and resolution so he may present these findings to the court.

Later in the week he is called to testify as the expert witness. The lawyer asks whether Dr. Ober has had an opportunity to meet with the couple. Dr. Ober responds to the court by confirming their meetings. The lawyer then asks him to review his findings for the courtroom and judge.

Dr. Ober explains his process of collecting information and informs the court that due to the absence of overt conflicts between them, he offered to conduct mediation with them for any remaining issues. He continues his testimony and further explains that any information collected during mediation is confidential. The judge compels him to give testimony.

Question to Consider in Forming a Plan of Action

Who is the client in this example?

- The court

To whom is confidentiality owed?

- No one

As a practitioner you have been referred a minor for treatment. Who is the client?

- The parents, the guardian, the legal parent(s) in a divorced couple
- What are the laws in your state concerning the communication of information to parents about a minor that may cause the damage to the therapeutic relationship?

You are working with an adult but a family member pays the bill each month. Who is the client?

- The adult

To whom is confidentiality owed?

- The adult

This chapter has presented a series of recommendations and examples to help you begin to think about risk management techniques. In whatever clinical position you find yourself, there will be questions that will be prudent to address in creating a plan of action. Be thoughtful, familiar with the evidence-based literature, trained in what you are about to do, and document your thinking in your progress notes as if you might need to defend yourself in court.

CHAPTER **2**

THE LEGAL SYSTEM

When we first set eyes on state and federal laws, statutes, common laws, and regulations, it can seem overwhelming. "Which one do I apply? What is the difference?" you may ask. A systematic way of looking at these definitions will make the descriptions and applications to the mental health field clear and simple.

A knowledge base for the workings of our legal system will make it easier to navigate. I will present this information in a simplistic format.

THE LAW

A State Law vs. a Federal Law

Federal law is created at the national level and applies to all states, including the District of Columbia. The laws are enacted either by Congress (House of Representatives and the Senate) or can also be made by the United States Supreme Court. Federal law is based on the U.S. Constitution.

One of the purposes of the constitution is to set constraints around governmental powers. The constitution protects the basic rights of every person living in the United States and its territories.

State law applies to each separate U.S. state and only that state. There are fifty states and several commonwealths and territories within the United States. Each has its own system of laws and courts that handle issues such as criminal matters, divorce and family matters, welfare, public assistance or Medicaid matters, and wills, to name a few.

The United States holds three territories: American Samoa and Guam in the Pacific Ocean and the U.S. Virgin Islands in the Caribbean Sea. Although they are governed by the United States, the territories do not have statehood status.

No state law may violate citizens' constitutional rights. However, if a state law affords a person more rights than federal law, the state law will prevail within that state. At the same time, if a state imposes more responsibility on its residents than the federal law, the state law prevails. If the state and federal laws are in obvious conflict, the federal law prevails.

For example, under the Health Insurance Portability and Accountability Act (HIPAA), medical records need to be kept for six years. HIPPA retention is from the date of its creation or the date when it last was in effect. But, for instance, California law requires that medical records be kept for clients for at least seven years. California affords clients greater protection of their health care information, thus California state law trumps federal law.

In other states, like Alabama, state law requires retention of records for five years. HIPPA's requirement is one year greater, so in this case federal law trumps Alabama law.

Each state may have different record retention laws that vary by setting or type of record. In addition, federal law payers and regulatory or accrediting agencies may have regulations governing record retention. For example, the veterans administration functions under federal guidance.

It is more common for a state to have several specific statutes governing different types of medical records and information. Every state has some form of legislation governing mental health records. These may take four different forms.

First, many states have laws governing the records of clients in state mental hospitals or mental health programs

Second, a number of states have laws governing the records of specific mental health practitioners, most commonly psychologists, social workers, and counselors. Colo. Rev. Stat. Ann. § 12-43-218, for example, requires client consent for any disclosure by a psychologist or psychotherapist, with no treatment exception.

Third, a number of states have specific statutes governing the records of clients who are involuntarily committed to mental institutions.

Fourth, most states have statutes that generally govern the records of mental health clients.

Most states also have statutes governing substance abuse records. The federal substance abuse treatment confidentiality law, 42 U.S.C. § 290dd-2, also independently governs some types of mental health records. This statute provides:

> *Records of the identity, diagnosis, prognosis, or treatment of any client which are maintained in connection with the performance of any program or activity relating to substance abuse education, prevention, training, treatment, rehabilitation, or research, which is conducted,*

regulated, or directly or indirectly assisted by any department or agency
of the United States shall, . . . be confidential and be disclosed only
for the purposes and under the circumstances expressly authorized. . .

The comparison between individual state law and HIPPA as it relates to mental health and substance abuse records will guarantee compliance.

Common (Case) Law vs. Statutes

Federal laws do not address all areas of law. In the cases where they do not cover particular instances, state or local laws will prevail.

Each state also has a constitution, which represents the highest legal power for that state. The state may enact their own laws called statutes, which then apply to everyone in that state. The legislative body of government for that state enacts that statute.

Common law, or "judge-made law," which it is a set of rules that derived from written decisions of judges who have heard lawsuits and legal arguments. Common law is often referred to as precedential law.

For example, the duty to warn, in some states, is statutory while in other states it is common law.

Some states have codified duties to warn, though duty to warn laws vary from state to state. Some states have permissive warning that allows mental health professionals to waive confidentiality discretionarily, but do not mandate it, and do not impose liability for failing to warn. Other states have not established any kind of statutory duty to warn, though it may be imposed by case law. Still other states are silent on both, for example, Nevada.

Elements of Law

An element is an essential legal requirement for a cause of action to be brought (the right to bring a lawsuit). Each action (negligence, breach of contract, trespass, assault, etc.) is made up of a basic set of these elements, which must be alleged and then proven.

Let's use an example to illustrate what the elements of a particular law entail.

You perused the newspaper in the morning. There was a report of a family driving cross-country in a van. The parents were in the front seat and the four children ranging in age from one to six were in the backseats. All were wearing their seatbelts.

There was a car accident. A drunk driver traveling at a high speed had plowed into the car. Three children and one of the parents were killed. The 1-year-old boy and his father survived.

You read that the drunk driver had been previously cited for driving under the influence. The driver is being charged with involuntary manslaughter. How could this happen when an entire family has been killed? You are outraged.

These charges are based on legal principles. Legal suits require elements.

An element is one part of a whole. In law, all the elements of the charges must be proven in a court of law to win a case.

Returning to the example for a moment, different state laws often separate charges of murder on the basis of severity and penalties. The key element in this case is intent.

The prosecuting attorney decides to charge the driver with involuntary manslaughter or, as it is also referred to, criminally negligent homicide.

At trial the prosecutor must prove each element. The main difference between murder and involuntary manslaughter is that murder generally encompasses the element of intent to kill or cause serious bodily harm while involuntary manslaughter does not.

While the motorist never intended to kill anyone, his or her negligence in operating a car while impaired is enough to meet the requirements of the charge.

Malpractice

A malpractice action falls under the laws of the state and is filed through legal channels. Malpractice is an act of negligence and also is composed of elements.

Legally it is what is called a tort action, which is an accusation of harm or a hurt. The individual is seeking monetary relief in civil court through legal channels. Malpractice is composed of four elements: duty of care, breach of the duty, causation, and damages.

Duty of care, in the field of mental health, means that a relationship has been formed between the therapist and the client for client care. The inherent assumption is that the health care practitioner must meet the best practice in which a reasonably prudent professional should exercise appropriate care in the same or similar circumstances.

A breach of duty of care means that the therapist acted in a negligent or improper manner or deviated from the best practice required to treat a client.

Causation is the breach of care done by the professional that either caused or contributed to causing harm to a client. Causation is a difficult concept to understand.

For example, a person injures her arm and is examined by a physician who overlooks the break on the x-ray. Weeks later since the person is still experiencing severe pain, she seeks another opinion. The x-ray clearly shows the broken bone. A cast is placed on the injured arm and it heals. There has been no damage. Causation has not been demonstrated.

In an alternative scenario, an individual complains of a pain in his lower back. He goes to a physician who does a perfunctory examination and diagnoses the problem as severe muscle strain. Six months later the pain persists and the person sees another health care provider. The new provider diagnoses the condition as lung cancer, and a year later the man dies. In this case, causation has been established.

Injury or harm has occurred and can be identified by the person. In addition, the harm should have been foreseeable given the actions of the care provider.

The defendant is seeking monetary damages from a civil court as a method of relief.

Emotional harm is hard to put a dollar value on. It is a difficult task for juries. The jury must also decide what it believes is appropriate compensation.

Any malpractice action requires an attorney. It is a suit heard in a civil court setting rather than a criminal court. Evidence is presented.

STANDARDS OF EVIDENCE

Evidence is information that is presented to a court that a reasonable person might accept as enough to support a conclusion.

There are three levels of evidence relevant to our discussion.

Preponderance of the Evidence

The preponderance-of-the-evidence standard is met if the judge or jury believes the evidence shows the defendant is more likely than not—more than 50% likely—to be responsible.

Clear and Convincing Evidence

Clear and convincing means the evidence is highly and substantially more likely to be true than not. The judge must reliably believe that the truth of the factual argument is highly probable.

Beyond a Reasonable Doubt

Beyond a reasonable doubt is the highest legal standard. It is the standard used for murder.

The evidence must be so convincing that no reasonable person would ever question the defendant's guilt. The standard requires that the evidence offer no logical explanation or conclusion other than that the defendant committed the crime.

Other notable differences are that criminal cases almost always allow for a trial by jury. Civil cases also allow jury decisions, but a judge may decide some civil lawsuits.

Additionally, a defendant in a criminal case is entitled to an attorney, and if he or she cannot afford one, the state must provide an attorney and incur the expense. A defendant in a civil case is not given an attorney and must independently pay for one or be pro se, which means that a person is representing himself or herself in court.

The protections afforded to defendants under criminal law are considerable because criminal cases can have greater consequences such as lengthy jail sentences in state prisons or even execution in some states.

We are witnessing a surge in the number of malpractice suits filed against mental health professionals. The reasons behind these trends are perplexing.

Case Example

* * * * * * * * * * *

A new female client is referred to you. She complains that she has felt hopeless for months. She feels her general outlook is bleak and although she feels as if you can't help, she has come to you as a last resort. The client had been an active member of a large social network filled with activities. The joy and meaning in these relationships has faded.

She complains that she has lost her appetite and is losing weight. She reports losing ten pounds in three weeks. In addition, she is always tired. She reports that she is waking up early in the morning and not able to fall back asleep. She describes her mood as irritable and her tolerance is low resulting in impatience and criticism of her work colleagues and dear friends.

She has trouble focusing and subsequently making decisions. During a business conference meeting her mind drifted off and she was embarrassed when she was asked a question and her mind went blank resulting in an uncomfortable silence in the meeting.

You have many years of experience and tend to be a practitioner who is open to using alternative strategies in helping clients. Your motto is Flexibility with whatever works.

After careful evaluation you surmise she may be suffering from depression. Your approach is unique. You have found that in your experience traditional treatments have not been effective and in a holistic journal, which is not peer reviewed, you have read about this method.

Your method is to wrap your clients in soft Polartec® blankets. You, of course, use pink for women and blue for men. You then ask your clients to roll themselves in the blanket on the floor. The clients look like they are in a papoose. You roll them around on the floor while cradling their heads to avoid a traumatic brain injury

After careful conversation with your client, you begin.

Your client is not improving. Given the increased intensity of her symptoms, she is now at risk of losing her job due to her mood fluctuations and absenteeism. She is short tempered and developing a pattern of continued lateness because she can't seem to gather herself in the mornings and get ready for her workdays. Rather than seeking out consultation, reading recent research, or seeking out supervision by a specialist in this field, you only decide to increase her sessions to twice a week.

She promptly gets fired and abruptly terminates treatment. Several months later you receive a notice from the court that you are being sued for negligence, a malpractice action. After a number of legal maneuvers, your time in court has arrived. You are on the stand and the plaintiff's attorney is inquiring as to your treatment history with the client.

This attorney then asks, "What is the best practice for depression?" You begin to reply by explaining your strategy. The attorney interrupts your answer and repeats the question. While you are answering, he strolls over to his assigned table in the courtroom and picks up some papers. He slowly strolls back, hands you the piece of paper, and asks that you read the contents to the court. The gist of the article is that the best practice for depression is medicine and psychotherapy.

This case does not imply that additional interventions are not helpful but rather what is the accepted best practice.

The jury finds against you and your damages are exorbitant. The standard of proof in states for a malpractice action varies between preponderance and clear and convincing, the two lowest standards.

Please keep in mind this example is simplified.

You are responsible for being up-to-date on the best practices through reviewing the literature, consultation with colleagues, and extensive clinical experience.

COMMON FORMS OF MENTAL HEALTH NEGLIGENCE AND RISK MANAGEMENT STRATEGIES

The shift over the past twenty years toward private mental health care has created increased avenues for plaintiffs to be remunerated for injuries caused by mental health professionals.

Mental health professionals are increasingly being held accountable for their negligence. Here are some of the most common forms of negligence complaints:

Failure to Conduct a Proper Suicide Risk Assessment

What factors should be considered?
- Demographics: age, gender, marital status, employment, and living arrangements
- Family history of suicide
- For adolescents, exposure to a friend's suicide
- Prior suicide attempts
- Presentation at time of assessment
- Diagnosis
- Major depressive disorder, bipolar disorder, and schizophrenia have the highest suicide completion rates.

- Does the client have a comorbid substance dependency or abuse disorder? (Both of which might markedly increase the risk for suicide.)
- Does the client have a persistent medical condition?
- Document all suicide risk assessments in the record.

If a clinician fails to perform or improperly performs an assessment, or if the clinician unreasonably underestimates the client's risk, the clinician may well be liable if the client commits or attempts to commit suicide.

On the other hand, courts are likely to be more forgiving towards clinicians if a client commits suicide without any prior warning.

I know of three suicides completed on an inpatient psychiatric unit even though the patients were watched by two staff members during their stay.

. . . .

Excessive or Inappropriate Self-disclosure

Self-disclosure can be used as a treatment technique, and many clinicians use self-disclosure at least occasionally.

Risk Management Strategy

Is the disclosure for the purposes of the client or for the purposes of the therapist?

Is the communication appropriate to be disclosed to a client with this type of mental health condition?

- *Example*: If a client has a history of sexual trauma it may be clinically useful to disclose that the therapist has experienced a situation similar to establish a degree of empathy. On the other hand, if a therapist is disclosing this information because of the therapist's own problems, it is not appropriate. This balance can be precarious.

. . . .

Business Relationships with Clients

Therapists have entered into relationships of a business nature with present or former clients.

Risk Management Strategy

- Don't do it—ever.

- There is an inherent unequal bargaining power between the therapist and client once a therapeutic relationship has been established. Entering into a business relationship with a present or former client may be viewed as exploitation.

• • • • • • • • • • • •

Using Techniques Without Proper Training

An ongoing problem has been the use of treatment techniques that therapists are not well trained in.

Risk Management Strategy

- A therapist should not use any techniques without being thoroughly trained and experienced in them. It is likely not a best practice to use a technique after only being trained in it one time.
- Example: Your therapist takes a day course in EMDR. Does this qualify them as an expert?

• • • • • • • • • • •

Using Incorrect Diagnosis Deliberately

Managed care and the term *medical necessity* has become a part of mental health jargon. There has been a rise in allegations that therapists are deliberately reporting diagnoses to insurance companies that are not accurate to trigger increased coverage for their clients.

Risk Management Strategy

- Diagnosis used for treatment and insurance purposes should be the same. There is not a separate one for treatment purposes and for billing insurance purposes. In a court of law, the existence of two different diagnoses challenge the therapist's veracity

• • • • • • • • • • •

Avoiding the Medical Model

The increased complexities of treatment including elements of informed consent, overwhelming changing of standards of care, keeping records, and introduction of better medicines have left some therapists perplexed and rejecting of the changing medical model of mental health treatment. They believe they should be held to different standards particularly with the alternative holistic models.

Risk Management Strategy

- This is equivalent to telling the IRS you don't believe in paying taxes and refusing to do so. The results won't be pretty!
- The medical model is the standard of care for serious and persistent mental illness.

• • • • • • • • • • •

Sexual Impropriety

Client sexual attraction, involvement, and intimacy.

Risk Management Strategy

- *DON'T HAVE SEX WITH YOUR CLIENTS EVER!!!!!!!!!*

• • • • • • • • • • •

Inadequate Notes

Failure of therapists to document accurate notes or write any notes at all.

Risk Management Strategy

- Identify information and reason for first contact.
- Relevant history and risk factors, medical status, and prior treatment records (if unsuccessful document efforts).
- Dates of service and fees. Insurance information if necessary.
- Diagnostic impressions, assessments, treatment plans, peer consultation, testing reports, and other relevant data progress notes. Information about treatments chosen and other treatments that might have been considered but rejected.
- Release of information documentation.
- Relevant telephone calls and out-of-office contacts.
- Follow-up efforts when clients have quit without prior discussion.
- Documentation of clear information in the event another practitioner takes over the delivery of services.

Failure to Obtain Peer Consultation

Separation of therapists from each other—with, for example, a fee for service model, or the independent private practice models has created isolation for practitioners with clinical judgments often made in isolation.

Risk Management Strategy

- Peer consultation provides not only collegial support but also feedback from other clinicians. Whenever recommendations are made, they should be documented.

• • • • • • • • • • •

Breach of Confidentiality

The duty of confidentiality prohibits a licensed mental health care provider from disclosing information about a client's case to others without permission.

Risk Management Strategy

- Providers and health care systems *must* take precautions to ensure that only authorized access to protected health information occurs.
- Client care often requires that information about clients be discussed among members of a health care team; all team members have authorized access to confidential information about the clients they care for.

• • • • • • • • • • •

Abandonment and Termination

Abandonment is not the same as treatment termination.
Abandonment is when a practitioner inappropriately ends treatment without notice.

Risk Management Strategy

- Practitioners may end the therapy if a client:
  - isn't benefiting from therapy;
  - may be harmed by the treatment;
  - no longer needs therapy; or
  - threatens the therapist, him- or herself, or others.
- Facilitate care to another provider.
- Include the client in the plan.

Information Communicated to a Client at the Onset of Treatment

Clients have the right to know the boundaries of treatment and the therapeutic relationship

Risk Management Strategy

- A practitioner must explain the limits of confidentiality:
    - Mandatory reporting
    - Danger to self or others by reason of mental illness
    - Inability to care for oneself caused by mental illness
- Explanation of the clinician's record keeping.
- The clinician's expertise, experience, and training.
- Alternative treatment or service approaches.
- Fees and billing practices.
- Client's contact in case of emergencies.
- Services a practitioner will provide and those they will not.

• • • • • • • • • • •

Informed Consent Was Not Obtained

Risk Management Strategy

- Obtain informed consent prior to agreeing to work with a client(s).
- Highlight important areas verbally with the client.
- Verbal consent is inadequate, written informed consent is required.

CHAPTER 3

WORKING WITH ATTORNEYS

As mental health practitioners we are afraid of attorneys. I have repeatedly heard colleagues ask if they can tell a client that they will not appear in court for them under any circumstances.

Most likely this response comes from both our lack of knowledge and understanding of what lawyers do. In this chapter I am going to describe not only the attorneys' role but also their tasks in a civil suit.

Our training as mental health practitioners has been focused on the development of relationships that are filled with empathy, insight, and stability. We want to create an environment that feels safe for people to talk about their fears, memories, and troubles. Seeking out mental health care still carries a stigma. One view is that we should be able to pull ourselves up by our bootstraps. I have often heard outsiders suggest to those suffering from depression that they should "get out of bed and participate in life, that will help." This misunderstanding forces those who have been hospitalized, taken medication or seen a therapist for psychiatric care to keep it secret. An Attorney's role is very different than a mental health practitioner's role.

What is an attorney?

An attorney represents a client and advises the client on his or her legal situation. This may be in individual cases, large companies to small disputes, every step along the way and through the court proceedings. It is the attorney's job to be a strong advocate for the client's interest. Attorneys may serve a host of different roles in court.

What does a criminal defense attorney do?

- Criminal lawyers work within the criminal justice system.
- If a prosecutor believes a crime was committed, he or she can press charges against the alleged criminal without the consent or cooperation of the victim.

- Defense attorneys represent alleged criminals, at the state's expense, if the defendant cannot afford one.

What does a civil attorney do?

- An injured party has to hire a civil lawyer.
- An attorney cannot bring about a negligence lawsuit. It is the party harmed (plaintiff) who decides to sue.
- Defendants in civil lawsuits must hire their own lawyers, at their own expense.
- In a civil lawsuit the attorney is seeking monetary damages as the remedy harm.

What are a lawyer's responsibilities in a civil action?

Declaration of Claims

A declaration is a formal notice about a plaintiff's statement of a claim against the defendant that sets out the facts and circumstances that make up the case in open court.

Your honor, my name is Mr. or Ms. Lawyer and I represent Mr./ Ms. Non-lawyer who has brought a negligence suit alleging she or he has been harmed by Dr. Therapist who had engaged in an inappropriate sexual relationship with him causing serious harm. We are seeking monetary remuneration for that harm caused by these actions.

The declaration gives the title of the action, the court and place of trial, the basis for the claim, and the relief sought.

Formal Notice

The other side has been served with a copy of the complaint or received through registered mail. This is called *service of process*.

Presentation of arguments of each party

- Questions and inquiry of the parties

Statement from the therapist

HIPAA creates national standards to protect an individual's medical records and personal health information (PHI),

States also have their own laws in place to protect PHI. Therefore, you must be familiar with your own state's guidelines as well as HIPPA.

Closing arguments

When I was in law school all students were required to take a yearlong trial advocacy course. These classes were taught by sitting judges. The course was to help us experience different roles that lawyers might play in court. So, over the yearlong course students pretended to be attorneys and judges, presented opening and closing arguments, and questioned witnesses.

When my turn came to do the closing arguments, the judge asked me to turn my back to the jury and then proceed with my statement. I thought, "You're kidding me." Of course I didn't share my thoughts. There are instances when arguments in court simulate a theater performance and it impacts the outcome.

We all still remember in the closing arguments of the defense in the criminal trial of O.J. Simpson, when the attorney said, "If the glove does not fit you must acquit." At the time of this text's publication in 2016, it has been twenty-one years since that statement and most of us still recall it.

Decision

A judge or jury examines the evidence to decide whether, by a "preponderance of the evidence" (standard of proof for civil suits), the defendant should be held legally responsible for the damages alleged by the plaintiff.

HOW DO WE AS MENTAL HEALTH
PRACTITIONERS DEAL WITH ATTORNEYS?

- Opposing counsels have different interests and agendas. Because you may see them having lunch together or chatting, you should not assume they are conversing or strategizing about the case from their different vantage points. Lunch is lunch.
- Lawyers are analytical and use legal reasoning to achieve their goals.
- Court involvement makes mental health practitioners nervous, and lawyers are skilled at using our anxiety as a tool to their advantage.
- Their task is to gather information to be used in a court of law. If the opposing lawyer questions you in any other place than the courtroom, limit the information. Mental health practitioners are trained to be helpful and empathic. Don't volunteer information because it can backfire.

In my work as an expert witness, I often find myself rushing to court to wait. Sometimes I am in a hallway waiting to be called as a witness. Perhaps, the judge doesn't want me to hear the testimony of the person on the stand testifying before me.

When you hang around court enough attorneys come to recognize you. You may even have worked with that attorney on some other cases. Chitchatting while waiting is not uncommon, including asking you questions about your thinking. What information you volunteer may affect the outcome of the case. Don't try to be helpful and empathetic, be quiet!

PAYMENT FOR LEGAL REQUESTS

Copies

There are times when a client might ask for copies of their records and you must reproduce them. You can charge for copies as long as you include a statement in your informed consent to that end. If you go to a hospital, for example, and want your electronic records, there is often a charge.

Summaries, Court Documents, Travel Fees, etc.

At any point prior to trial, a client or lawyer may ask for treatment records. Depending on your progress note entries, it may make more sense to submit a treatment summary. It is an arduous process to put one together. The cost of this activity is at the discretion of the provider, but I would recommend taking a retainer, which is, simply advanced payment.

There may be other requests such as preparation time, phone calls, depositions, time required in giving testimony, mileage, attorneys' fees, and costs incurred by the therapist as a result of the legal action, court appearances, etc. Fees should be set in advance and stated in your informed consent.

Resisting Disclosure

When a client refuses to sign a consent for release of information for court, you will need to resist the disclosure on behalf of the client. The practitioner will need an independent attorney to defend the confidentiality of the client and his or her records. Clients should be informed that they would be responsible for those legal fees. You might want to include this piece of information in the informed consent that you use with all patients.

FORMAL DEMANDS IN THE CONTEXT OF LITIGATION

Perry Mason is one of those wonderful television series that is eternal. The story usually had the ever-talented private investigator, Paul, finding evidence and whispering his findings to Perry Mason while the last witness was on the stand under examination. With a nod, Perry would confront the witness and begin by saying, "Isn't it true. . ." and then he would explain to the court what he believed had actually occurred. The witness would end up confessing while on the stand, and the case was solved. Not in real life!

Prior to the start of any trial, there is a protracted period of time during which each side can find out or "discover" a great deal of information about the other side's allegations and the supporting evidence. Formal demands in the context of litigation are how this information is obtained.

Court Orders and Subpoenas

A *subpoena* is a request for the production of documents or a request to appear in court or another legal proceeding in person.

A subpoena issued by someone other than a judge or clerk magistrate, such as a court clerk or an attorney, is not a court order.

There are some states, such as South Carolina, Florida, and Pennsylvania, where attorneys who take the oath of office are considered to be officers of the court. They may issue court orders. Make sure you check your state law so that you know when a subpoena carries the weight of the court.

The subpoena request may be delivered in a number of ways:
- Hand-delivered
- E-mailed (receipt acknowledgment requested)
- Certified mail (return receipt requested); or
- Hearing it read aloud in court.

A subpoena is a lawyer's assertion that he or she is entitled to the requested information.

A court order has determined that the lawyer is entitled to the information. A court order typically has *order* typed on it and is signed by a judge or magistrate. It will likely contain some words that explain that one party has brought a motion (request) to compel another party to provide documents or testimony in court. The court has considered that motion and is now ordering the requested information.

A court order trumps HIPPA.
HIPAA trumps a court clerk's signature.

In the attempt to gather as much information as possible, subpoenas are sometimes drafted to look like court orders, when they have actually only been signed by a court clerk. These subpoenas are not court orders.

Lawyers use this as a shortcut to get patient health information. Be wary. If the document you have been served is **NOT** an actual court order and you release the patient information without proper consent, you could find yourself in violation of HIPAA, with hefty fines for the breach of information.

If you receive consent from your client, be sure that the consent covers the information the subpoena is seeking, nothing more.

If you are in a court hearing and the judge verbally orders you to divulge information, this is also a court order that must be obeyed.

If you are not certain whether the document is a subpoena or court order, you can contact the clerk of the court.

A *subpoena duces tecum* is used to compel the production of documents that are admissible before the court. It cannot be used to require oral testimony or affirm the truth of the documents; it is merely to bring documents into the court.

The easiest strategies for responding to a subpoena might include making contact with the attorney issuing the document. Advise and consult with your client. Clients often sign releases without knowing what they are signing them for.

When was the last time you went to rent a car? The attendant gives you papers over the counter and you sign them. I have never heard anyone say, "I am going over to sit down and read it all, I'll return in two hours."

Document, document, document!

I want to list for you some suggestions that might be useful in considering how to reply to a subpoena.

The first step is reading the subpoena, **NOT** complying with it.

You need to take the time and carefully review what the document is requesting of you. You may turn over information only if the subpoena qualifies as a court order. If you have verified that it is a court order, you may turn over the documents or testify without obtaining your client's consent.

Typically, a court order will be identified as such on the first page. In addition, a judge, not a judge's clerk or an attorney, will sign the document, except for the exceptions mentioned previously.

If the document is not a court order, you will need to obtain your client's consent before releasing any confidential information. The easiest route to get information is simply to verbally request it. Both state and federal jurisdictions recognize the psychotherapist-patient privilege.

This privilege allows a client to prevent confidential material from being disclosed to others and in court. When obtaining this consent, you should tell your client exactly what specific information you have been asked to turn over and be clear that once it is turned over there is no guarantee that the information will subsequently be kept confidential. You have no control over how the information is utilized.

If you object and want the court to acknowledge your reluctance you will need to file a *motion to quash*. Typically, a motion to quash contains a request to the court asking to modify or terminate the subpoena based on certain stated objections. For example, if the information requested would harm your client in some way, a motion to quash might be a path to take. The client's attorney could file this motion.

Another possibility is to seek a protective order for the information.

I received a subpoena to give information to the court to testify about the level of dangerousness of an individual when he was not taking his medication. I had seen him three years earlier when he did stop his medicine and got arrested for stealing from a car. I contacted the attorney and related that since I hadn't seen him in all that time I had no knowledge of his mental status at the time of the request.

A written consent that you obtain for the release of information should include, at the very least, specifically what information will be disclosed, to whom this information will be disclosed to and the purpose of the disclosure, and the signature of the client and date.

If any of these options are not applicable to your circumstances, you should seek additional guidance from your own attorney.

We are obligated not to reveal that we have ever known or treated the client. The fact that you are treating a client is protected health information under HIPPA guidelines.

One way to communicate this information is say that you cannot affirm or deny whether you have provided treatment to the person named. But if you had, then you could not legally or ethically release such information without an order from a judge or an authorization from the client.

DISCOVERY

When I travel on Southwest Airlines, the flight attendants' instructions given before takeoff are crystal clear. They might say, "If you have a larger electronic device, it will have an on-off switch. You have two choices, to have it on or off. Choose off." Simple.

Discovery is simple in that way as well. Discovery is discovery.

Discovery refers to a phase of litigation where each party seeks information from the other. Information requested (discovered) can be very broad.

Another important component of discovery is that just because the information sought may be inadmissible in a court of law does not exempt it from being introduced during the discovery process. What this means is that any party to litigation may have to place much of their past personal lives onto the public record.

Previously, if a woman accused someone of rape, a woman's sexual history could be asked about in court. The intention was to compromise the victim's character. Rape shield laws now protect this line of questioning.

Courts have gradually recognized that there are some aspects of personal life that should remain private, beyond the lawyer's reach. This might include issues such as health or body issues, sexuality, sexual practices, or sexual partners, spiritual or religious beliefs or immediate family relationships.

Why do we have discovery instead of just requesting the information be directly admitted into the courtroom? Discovery narrows the issues of a lawsuit. It allows parties to get evidence that would not be available to either person for use during a trial. In this way relevant information may be introduced later at trial since the process of discovery is under oath. Courts are fact-finding institutions, which allow access to all material facts (information relevant for the trial).

Imagine if all the information for a trial had to be presented in court prior to the beginning of the trial. Then the court had to sift through all that information and select which pieces of information were important to the case. The trial process would essentially grind to a halt.

Discovery procedures promote settlement. Since both parties have the same information prior to a trial, the strength of each case can be evaluated prior to the beginning of a court hearing.

General Motors agreed to pay $900 million as part of a Justice Department investigation into its failure to fix a deadly ignition-switch defect blamed for more than 120 deaths. GM also admitted to having defrauded customers by marketing its vehicles as safe.

Toyota paid $1.2 billion in connection with its handling of an unintended acceleration problem in its cars that resulted in the deaths of drivers. Toyota agreed to pay this staggering sum to avoid prosecution for covering up severe safety problems that the company knew were deadly.

As part of the agreement Toyota was forced to admit to consumers that it concealed evidence and made deceptive statements about safety-related issues.

A settlement offer may be made to avoid not only a lengthy expensive trial, but also the possibility of higher damages that a jury may award. Money!

Another recent example was the case against Walmart by the actor-comedian Tracy Morgan who was injured in a car crash. His limousine bus was stopped when a Walmart truck slammed into the still vehicle at a high rate of speed, 25 mph over the 45 mph speed limit. The bus driver had been driving fourteen hours nonstop. The accident set off a chain-reaction collision that eventually involved six vehicles and twenty-one people.

Initially Walmart blamed Morgan for not wearing his seat belt. When additional information was obtained during discovery, rather than risk a lengthy costly trial, Walmart decided to settle out of court. The agreement is, of course, confidential as they often are.

Any tidbit of information that might have the slightest link to the lawsuit is fair inquiry for discovery. Understandably this enormous range of material gathering sometimes leads to abuse. Lawyers might try to pry into areas that have no legitimate significance for the lawsuit. They may pursue private and confidential information with the sole goal of embarrassing the parties.

The four types of discovery tools that are often used in lawsuits are depositions; requests for production of evidence; interrogatories; and requests for admission. Following are the benefits of each.

DEPOSITIONS

In a deposition, one party's lawyer conducts face-to-face questioning of the other party or a witness to the dispute. The person being questioned, the deponent, must answer under oath. The answers are recorded for later use at trial. If the deponent is not available to testify at the trial later for whatever reasons, information obtained from discovery can be read to the jury as evidence.

If the deponent does testify and gives different answers in court than were given during deposition, the questions and answers can be used to show the jury that the witness changed the story and this leaves open the question of the veracity of the witness's testimony.

REQUESTS FOR PRODUCTION OF EVIDENCE

During this procedure one party asks the other for physical evidence related to the dispute. It is a method to collect pertinent documents that may include signed informed consents or medical records or other documents related to the issue.

These requests can also be used to inspect physical objects or property.

INTERROGATORIES

Interrogatories are written questions one party sends to the other to be answered under oath. The answers can be used at trial in the same way as deposition answers. It is often a series of short questions that are limited in the information gathered.

Insurance companies often use this approach to get information from a driver who has caused an accident. It is the least expensive method.

REQUESTS FOR ADMISSION

One party asks the other party to admit, under oath, that certain facts are true or certain documents are genuine. It is under this procedure that medical records are admitted. Authentication is the process of determining whether someone or something is who or what it is declared to be. Records are self-authenticating and do not require the authentication procedure be conducted in court.

Under the law, hearsay is an out of court statement made by a declarant for the truth of the matter. Information received from other people cannot be adequately substantiated.

Medical records contain information that has been received from other people that cannot adequately be substantiated. The medical record gets into the court proceeding as an exception to the hearsay rule.

Here are some of the things lawyers often ask for in discovery:

- Anything a witness or party saw, heard, or did in connection with the dispute.
- Anything anyone said at a particular time and place (for example, in a business meeting related to the dispute or after a car accident that turned into a lawsuit).

- The identity of anyone who might know something about the dispute or about the injuries or money losses suffered by either party.

- Detailed information on how a business is run. (For example: a party might try to determine how a company that sold a dangerous product decided what to sell, documents relating to the dispute). The most recent example is the clinic where the comedian Joan Rivers went to undergo a minor office procedure (endoscopy) and was given anesthesia. She died from cardiac arrest and the family sued the clinic for negligence.

- Personal, educational, and professional background of a witness.

LIMITATIONS ON WHAT CAN BE DISCOVERED

Confidential Conversations

Conversations between people engaged in particular relationships receive a special legal protection known as privilege. No one can be required to disclose any information, whether verbal or written, that was confidentially exchanged within the following relationships:

- Husband and wife
- Lawyer and client
- Doctor and patient
- Licensed mental health provider and client
- Religious advisor and advisee (any confidential conversation between a member of the clergy of a recognized religion and a person seeking spiritual counsel)

In some states, given the recent sex abuse charges within the Catholic Church, these parameters have changed. For example, the clergy are now mandated reporters of child sexual abuse in some states. State laws may differ on this issue.

Keeping Discovery Information from the Public

Even if a party is required to disclose certain information to the other side in a lawsuit, a court can treat information confidentially—that is, the party who receives it can be prevented from revealing it to anyone else, and the court can keep it out of the public record. To ensure this is the case, a judge usually mandates a protective order to keep the information confidential.

Finally, there are two types of witnesses in court; an expert and a fact witness. A witness who is qualified as an expert has special knowledge, skill, experience, training, or education. The expert may form an opinion and testify to it in court. A number of criteria must be met in order for the court to view someone as an expert. These include:

- The expert's scientific, technical, or other specialized knowledge will help the trier of fact to understand the evidence or to determine a fact in issue.
- The testimony is based on sufficient facts or data.
- The testimony is the product of reliable principles and methods.
- The expert has reliably applied the principles and methods to the facts of the case.

These characteristics alone do not make someone an expert; it is the court that adjudicates someone an expert based on the criteria mentioned previously.

Sometimes individuals have testified so often in court and are known to the court and the attorneys present that lawyers will stipulate to the person's expertise. In high-visibility cases, the lawyers may carefully question an expert on that person's qualifications to either have him or her rendered an expert or exclude that person from the expert role depending on the attorney's needs.

A fact witness may only testify to the facts. If you have been called as a fact witness and requested to use your expertise to render an opinion, it is important to clarify your role as a fact witness to maintain your credibility.

CHAPTER 4

FIDUCIARY CONTRACTS

In a fiduciary relationship, one person relies in confidence, good faith, and trust in another. Their aid, advice, or protection is sought. The fiduciary acts at all times for the sole benefit and in the best interest of the one who trusts. A fiduciary duty is the highest standard of care that we in the mental health field are tasked with.

The psychotherapist-patient contract, which is fiduciary, allows the practitioner to establish a legally binding business relationship with the patient. The subsequent breach of such a contract may lead to malpractice lawsuits or licensing complaints. The purpose is to satisfy ethical guidelines and is a useful and powerful risk management strategy.

How do you know you have a legally binding contract? As we discussed earlier on legal requirements, contracts are also made up of elements. All must be present for a contract to be legally binding.

There are five elements necessary to create a legal binding contract. There is an offer, an acceptance in strict compliance with the terms of the offer, a legal purpose or objective to the contract, a mutuality of obligation, consideration, and competence.

For an offer to be valid there must be a definite, clearly stated offer to do something. When an individual schedules a first meeting with a mental health practitioner (in any setting), the two parties are merely declaring a willingness to consider the possibilities. An agreement is not created if there is an acceptance of only the invitation to treat.

Acceptance can only be to what is offered. It establishes the terms and conditions of a contract. Acceptance can be given verbally, in writing, or inferred by action such as nodding your head (implied).

The contract requires that the parties intend to enter into a legally binding agreement. Parties who enter into the contract must understand that law can enforce the agreement. A contract for illegal distribution of drugs is not a binding contract because the purpose for which it exists is not legal. If you were to enter into a contract for the sale of marijuana in Colorado, would that be a legally binding contract?

The third element is referred to as mutuality of obligation. It is also known as a meeting of the minds. It is both parties' mutual understanding and assent to the expression of their agreement. This avoids the problem of one party to the contract declaring at some later time that it didn't understand what the agreement was all about.

Consideration is necessary for any binding contract to be valid. Consideration consists of either a benefit to the promisor or a detriment to the promisee. Up until the early 1990s some disciplines were not permitted to barter for services. However, there are many cultures where this is considered a valid form of payment. As long as it is neither exploitative nor harmful to a client, this has become an accepted form of payment. Mostly we transact business with money.

Finally, parties to a contract must be competent to enter into that contract. How do we determine competency? Many practitioners who work with the elderly population are sometimes concerned, for example, their client may be in the early stages of undiagnosed dementia since they appear cognitively limited. We may alter our presentation of the information to make it easier to understand.

Many clinicians assume that when they verbally give instructions that the competency of understanding may be demonstrated by repeating the parameters of the contract in their own words back to the speaker. Paraphrasing the instructions is also used. If that is to no avail, either we will not continue or proceed nonetheless.

Competency is always assumed unless a court has adjudicated otherwise. It is a legal description not a psychiatric one. The psychiatric term we use is *capacity*. Capacity to understand, to communicate, or general mental abilities.

Case Example

A priest was hospitalized in a forensic psychiatric unit.
He was charged with multiple counts of molesting young boys.
He had left the country for thirty years, which stopped the
statute of limitations on rape. Upon his return multiple charges

were leveled. There was some concern about his loss of memory
due to his age and mental status.

It was during a turbulent time for the Catholic Church,
and the publicity around other cases had already harmed
the church. The church hired exceptional experts including
a neurologist, a neuropsychologist, a psychiatrist as well as a
psychopharmacologist. All were tasked with evaluating the
priest and to give testimony in court. I had been assigned to do
a forensic evaluation and also give testimony.

Each of the experts gave impressive testimony and made
statements that in their professional opinions he was not
competent. I testified that I believed that this man, though
compromised, did in fact maintain a competency-based skill
set, understanding that the final determination was a judicial
one. All the other testimony by the experts was excluded because
competency is not a psychiatric decision but a legal finding by
the court.

For me one of the most difficult aspects of treatment is the monetary negotiation. As we know when we are contracted with the insurance panels, we must follow their guidelines; one of which is not waiving the copay.

If you don't bring up the exchange of money early on, it can be problematic. Imagine you have waited until the last moment to address paying. The meeting time with your client is drawing to a close and you remind the client of the required payment or co-pay. The client pulls out a checkbook. As the client is slowly writing out the check, he or she is talking about issues that the client may have neglected to mention during the session. Thirty minutes later, you are wrapping up and you compromised your and all the other patients' schedules.

The exchange of payment is part of a contractual agreement. Make a decision when you wish to be paid and be consistent. It would be prudent to add this information into an informed consent so it is clear.

When you go to the hospital for day surgery the first contact you have is with the billing department to make sure you can pay. I have never had one of these individuals say to me, "I recognize you must be nervous about your upcoming operation so we won't discuss payment now. After the procedure just go home to recuperate. When you feel better, give us a call and we'll settle the bill then if you like."

Remember, the money discussion is included in the fiduciary relationship you have with your client.

There are situations where your client may accumulate debt. I would certainly recommend against a situation like this, but it may inadvertently happen. I was always taught that I had to absorb the debt. This is incorrect. You have the right to use the services of a debt collection agency or go to small claims court if you have included this information in your informed consent.

It is not as if you contact a debt collection agency and announce that your client has been raped by all the men in her life and she had the poor judgment to marry a rapist as well! The information released is only the client's name, phone number, and amount owed.

While it is legal to use the services of a collection agency, these clients do have a higher rate of malpractice suits, either because of the type of client who doesn't pay bills may also be more litigious. Given these concerns, I generally recommend this as a last resort.

Finally, in relation to money, an individual's financial circumstances are constantly fluctuating. Since you are serving in a fiduciary role, any changes in a client's status must be renegotiated. It is not necessary to go through all the previously collected monetary information. You have the option to add a codicil to the consent. A codicil is often what is added to a will to change sections rather than rewriting the entire document from the beginning.

For example, Aunt Jane whom you are indebted to has raised you. In executing your will, you leave your entire estate to her as a way to say thank you. Over your life, you learn that Aunt Jane is actually a liar, fake, opportunistic, exploiting individual who has no morals. Rather than rewriting the entire document, you may add a codicil excluding her from the inheritance you originally intended.

When I call an attorney for advice I try to speak rapidly. It is well known that if you go over fifteen minutes you will be charged for half an hour. Other attorneys charge in ten-minute chunks of time. If that is a policy you want to implement, make sure it is included in your informed consent document.

Whatever information you want your client to know, be clear and concise and include it in your informed consent as part of developing a fiduciary relationship with your client.

I have noticed more recently that there is a sign in my dentist's office that says if I don't give twenty-four-hours' notice of a cancellation I will be charged $50.00. What is your policy about late cancellation or emergencies?

I have a twenty-four-hour cancellation policy that is clearly stated in my informed consent. An emergency is not six grandmothers dying over the course of the week. It is not a call five minutes before the session begins that someone has been nauseous throughout the night. My reply to that kind of a statement might be, "I have a bathroom next door to my office, feel free to step out if you feel unwell."

On the other hand, there are extenuating circumstances that may inhibit patients from coming to their appointments. For example, One day there was an enormous snowfall in Massachusetts. This was a private practice day for me. Massachusetts has the best snowplows on the face of this earth. Side roads were open as were schools and public transportation. I went trudging to my office. No one showed up and no one called.

Finally, one client contacted me to reschedule and commented that it was her assumption, given the weather conditions, that I had cancelled all my appointments. Do I charge each person for a missed appointment?

In my informed consent I state that exceptions can be made with the consent between the therapist and patient. This leaves me the latitude to alter certain policies. I thought to myself, "What could be more important to someone than a therapy appointment?" Not!

It turned out it was my poor estimation of the difficulties others had in coming to my office that day. I thought that clients should have called, but I also understood why people might have thought it was reasonable not to come based on the difficulty traveling. I opted to waive all fees. Having a statement in my informed consent that I reserve the right to make exceptions allowed me to do something differently without changing the terms of the contract.

Case Example

I never forget anything! I was seeing a young female client who was very reliable. She was always early for her appointments. If she needed to cancel or change the time, she called way in advance. Her parents had always been irresponsible with money. They had declared bankruptcy a number of times. She wanted to conduct her life differently and struggled to that end. She had been hired into a responsible position. She arrived on time, left on time, and worked throughout the day unlike some of us who play on the Internet when time permits.

*One evening she missed her appointment without calling.
I immediately called her. Of course, no one answers a phone
in the twenty-first century so I left a message. Later in the
evening she telephoned me to let me know she forgot the time.
Given that payment guidelines are in my informed consent,
I certainly was within the parameters to charge her. I opted
not to since I thought it was contraindicated for her treatment.
Without the clause about exceptions I would have been in
violation of our contractual agreement.*

If you decide to make exceptions for clients on an individual basis, make sure your consent addresses that. You do not want to be in a court of law with an attorney questioning you about favoritism because you follow one set of rules with one person and another with someone else.

What information might you include in an informed consent document? Below are some suggestions.

PSYCHOTHERAPEUTIC SERVICES

- Psychotherapy is difficult to explain in general statements. It can vary. There are many different methods the clinician may use to deal with the problems you bring to our meeting. Psychotherapy requires an effort on your part.

- Psychotherapy can have also have benefits and risks. Since therapy often involves discussing unpleasant aspects of your life, you may experience uncomfortable feelings like sadness, guilt, anger, and frustration, to mention a few. The intention of psychotherapy is for your benefit. But, there are no guarantees of what you will experience.

- Our first few sessions will include an evaluation of your needs. I will be able to offer you some first impressions of what our work will include, if you decide to continue with therapy. You should evaluate this information along with your own opinions and decide if you feel comfortable working with me.

- Therapy involves a large commitment of time, money, and energy, so you should be very careful about the therapist you select.

- If you have any questions we should discuss them whenever they arise. I will be happy to facilitate a referral to another mental health professional if that is what you decide.

MEETINGS

- Once psychotherapy begins, I will usually schedule one XX-minute session per week at a time we agree on. Sessions may be longer or more frequent depending on the agreement between us.

- Once an appointment hour is scheduled, you will be expected to pay for it unless you provide XX hours/days advance notice of cancellation, unless we both agree that you were unable to attend due to circumstances beyond your control. In unusual circumstances exceptions can be made with a discussion between us.

PROFESSIONAL FEE

- My hourly fee is $XX.

- In addition to weekly appointments, I charge $XX for other professional services you may need. I will break down the hourly cost if I work for periods of less than one hour. Other services include report writing, telephone conversations lasting longer than XX minutes, attendance at meetings with other professionals you have authorized, preparation of records or treatment summaries, and the time spent performing any other service you may request of me.

- If you become involved in legal proceedings that require my participation, you will be expected to pay for my professional time even if I am called to testify by another party. Since legal involvement is time consuming, I charge $XX per hour for preparation and attendance at any legal proceeding.

BILLING AND PAYMENT

- You will be expected to pay for each session at the time of each session unless we agree otherwise or unless you have insurance coverage that might require another arrangement. Payment schedules for other professional services will be agreed to when they are requested. (*In circumstances of unusual financial hardship, I may be willing to negotiate a fee adjustment or payment installment plan*).

- If your account has not been paid for more than 60 days and arrangements for payment have not been agreed on, I have the option to use legal means to secure the payment. This may involve hiring a collection agency or going through small claims court. If such legal action is necessary, its costs will be included in the claim. Your confidentiality will be maintained other than your name, the nature of services provided, and the amount due.

- I will, of course, give you the option to pay before any action is taken.

INSURANCE REIMBURSEMENT

- It is important to evaluate what resources you have available to pay for your treatment. If you have a health insurance policy, it will usually provide some coverage for mental health treatment. I will fill out forms and provide you with whatever assistance I can.

- Due to the rising costs of health care, insurance benefits have become more complex.

- You should also be aware that most insurance companies require you to authorize me to provide them with a clinical diagnosis. Sometimes I have to provide additional clinical information such as treatment plans or summaries, or copies of the entire record. This information will become part of the insurance company's files. Though all insurance companies claim to keep such information confidential, I have no control over what they do with it once it is in their hands. In some cases, they may share the information with a national medical information databank. I will provide you with a copy of any report I submit, if you request it.

- You always have the right to pay for my services yourself [unless prohibited by a contract].

CONTACT

- I am often not immediately available by telephone. When I am unavailable, my telephone is answered by an answering service [machine, voice mail] that I monitor frequently. I will make every effort to return your call on the same day you make it. If you are difficult to reach, please inform me of some times when you will be available.

- If you are unable to reach me and feel that you can't wait for my return call, please either go to or consult with the nearest emergency room. If I will be unavailable for an extended time, I will provide you with the name of a colleague to contact in my absence.

PROFESSIONAL RECORDS

- The laws and standards of my profession require that I keep treatment records. You are entitled to receive a copy of your records.

MINORS

- If you are under (age of majority in your state), the law may provide your parents/guardians the right to examine your treatment records.
- If I feel there is a high risk that you will seriously harm yourself or someone else. I will notify your parents/guardians of my concern. Before giving them any information, I will discuss the matter with you, if possible, and do my best to handle any objections you may have.

CONFIDENTIALITY

- In general, the law protects the privacy of all communications between a patient and a licensed practitioner. I can only release information with your written permission. But there are a few exceptions.
- In most legal proceedings, you have the right to prevent me from providing any information about your treatment. A judge may order my testimony without your consent.
- There are some situations in which I am legally obligated to take actions to protect others from serious bodily harm even if I have to reveal some information about a patient's treatment. I [whatever your state law requires to discharge my duty]. These may include notifying the potential victim, contacting the police, or seeking hospitalization for the patient. If a patient threatens to harm himself or herself, I may be obligated to seek hospitalization for him or her or to contact family members or others who can help provide protection.
- If I believe that a child, elderly person, or disabled person] is being abused, I am required by law to file a report with the appropriate state agency.
- I may occasionally find it helpful to consult with other professionals. During a consultation, I make every effort to avoid revealing your identity. The consultant is also legally bound to keep the information confidential. I will tell you about these consultations.

- Your signature below indicates that you have read the information in this document and agree to abide by its terms during our professional relationship.

MENTAL HEALTH PARITY

Paul Wellstone, a senator from Minnesota, was key in crafting the mental health parity laws. When his older brother, Stephen Wellstone, was a freshman in college, he suffered a severe mental breakdown. He spent the next two years in mental hospitals. Eventually, he recovered. But it took his parents twenty years to pay off the bills from those two years. Senator Wellstone was killed in a plane crash in 2002. The Paul Wellstone and Pete Domenici Mental Health Parity and Addiction Equity Act (MHPAEA) was enacted in October 2008.

What Is Mental Health Parity or Equal Coverage Laws?

Parity, in relation to mental health and substance abuse, prohibits insurers or health care service plans from discriminating between coverage offered for serious mental illness, substance abuse, and other physical disorders and diseases.

In short, parity requires insurers to provide the same level of benefits for mental illness, serious mental illness, or substance abuse as for other physical disorders and diseases. These benefits include visit limits, deductibles, copayments, and lifetime and annual limits. Parity only applies to insurance plans for public and private sector employers with over fifty employees.

Parity laws contain different variables that affect the level of coverage required under the law. Some state parity laws provide broad coverage for all mental illnesses. Other state parity laws limit the coverage to a specific list of biologically based (also referred to as medical necessity) or serious mental illnesses.

The state laws that are full parity provide equal benefits, to varying degrees, for the treatment of serious mental illness and biologically based mental illness, and may include treatment for substance abuse. The new federal parity law affects insurance policies that already provide some mental health coverage; there is no federal law directly mandating parity to the same extent as state laws.

Insurers must provide specific information and reasons in the event that reimbursement or payment for treatment is denied. For example, if a policy allows unlimited visits for diabetes, that same criteria would be applicable to the mental illness of schizophrenia.

State Parity Laws

If a state has a stronger state parity law, then health insurance plans regulated in that state must follow those laws. For example, if state law requires plans to cover mental health conditions, then they must do so, even though federal parity makes inclusion of any mental health benefits optional. In this circumstance, once again the state provides greater protections for clients therefore state law trumps federal law.

Federal parity replaces state law only in cases where the state law "prevents the application" of federal parity requirements. For example, if a state law requires some coverage for mental health conditions, then the federal requirement of equal coverage will trump the "weaker" state law.

Why Is Mental Health Parity Important?

Mental health parity laws define, for the most part, what is considered a biological-based mental illness or an illness that meets the requirements for medical necessity as defined by the states. The definition of biological illness and guidelines to qualify vary by state. There are some states that use the DSM. Other states use a different descriptive method.

Some states have laws that are specific to the state while others follow federal guidelines. You must know your state's requirements.

> *As practitioners, we know that the primary diagnosis that is given to an individual often determines the amount of sessions a person is entitled to. Because of this, it is tempting to use one of the more severe diagnoses to ensure the most extensive treatment possible. This is a fraudulent practice.*

The Affordable Care Act provides one of the largest expansions of mental health and substance use disorder coverage in a generation, by requiring that most individual and small employer health insurance plans, including all plans offered through the Health Insurance Marketplace cover mental health and substance use disorder services. Also required are rehabilitative and habilitative services that can help support people with behavioral health challenges.

The following are examples of what mental health parity laws might cover.

- Inpatient in-network and out-of-network services
- Outpatient in-network and out-of-network services
- Intensive outpatient services
- Partial hospitalization
- Residential treatment
- Emergency care
- Prescription drugs
- Co-pays
- Deductibles
- Maximum out-of-pocket limits

In addition, states are increasingly encouraging or requiring health plans to reimburse for telehealth services to ensure access to health care, including enacting or broadening the applicability of telehealth parity laws. This will allow individuals in rural counties to receive mental health care. Washington, Arkansas, New York, Colorado, Nevada, Minnesota, and Indiana have enacted limited telehealth parity laws recently.

CHAPTER 5

HIPPA GUIDELINES

The Health Insurance Portability and Accountability Act of 1996 (HIPAA; Pub. L. No. 104–191, 110 Stat. 1936, enacted August 21, 1996) was enacted by the US Congress and signed by President Bill Clinton in 1996.

HIPPA guidelines can be complex to understand. Whether you are in private practice or work with an organization, HIPPA guidelines apply to you.

In this chapter I will provide you with the information you need to know to meet the requirements of this federal law.

HIPAA guidelines set the standard for protecting patient data. Anyone or any institution that deals with protected health information (PHI) must ensure that all the required physical, network, and other security measures are in place and followed.

This includes:

- Anyone who provides treatment, payment, and operations in health care.
- Anyone with access to patient information and provides support in treatment, payment, or operations.
- Subcontractors must also be in compliance.

There are several components of this law for the protection of health care information that are important:

- Physical safeguards that include limited and authorized access in place. All covered entities, or companies that must be HIPAA compliant, must have policies about use and access to workstations and electronic media.
- Technical safeguards to allow only those authorized to gain access to electronic protected health data. Hospitals that use electronic records have set up systems such that only the psychiatric health care providers involved in the case can access the behavioral records.

- Tracking logs could be implemented to keep records of activity. An example might be sign-out sheets for paper records or guidelines that include access to records be confined to a designated place such as a nursing station or office of some sort.

- Technical policies should also cover the integrity controls, or measures put in place to secure all PHI. Electronic media errors or failures can be quickly remedied and data can be recovered accurately.

- Network, or transmission, security protects against unauthorized access. This includes all methods of transmitting data, such as e-mail or the Internet in general.

I have provided two samples of HIPPA compliant consents for authorization of the release of confidential information:

HIPAA Privacy Authorization Form

** Authorization for Use or Disclosure of Protected Health Information (Required by the Health Insurance Portability and Accountability Act, 45 C.F.R. Parts 160 and 164)

1. Authorization

   I authorize _____ (health care provider) to use and disclose the protected health information described below to _____ (individual seeking the information).

2. Effective Period

   This authorization for release of information covers the period of health care from:

   a. (Date) _____ to (Date) _____. or

   b. ☐ all past, present, and future periods.

3. Extent of Authorization

   a. ☐ I authorize the release of my complete health record (including records relating to mental health care, communicable diseases, HIV or AIDS, and treatment of alcohol or drug abuse), or

   b. ☐ I authorize the release of my complete health record with the exception of the following information:
   - Mental health records
   - Communicable diseases (including HIV and AIDS)
   - Alcohol/drug abuse treatment
   - Other (please specify): _____

4. This medical information may be used by the person I authorize to receive this information for medical treatment or consultation, billing or claims payment, or other purposes as I may direct.

5. This authorization shall be in force and effect until _____ (date or event), at which time this authorization expires.

6. I understand that I have the right to revoke this authorization, in writing, at any time.

7. I also understand that a revocation is not effective if any person or entity has already acted in reliance on my authorization or if my authorization was obtained as a condition of obtaining insurance coverage and the insurer has a legal right to contest a claim.

8. I understand that my treatment, payment, enrollment, or eligibility for benefits will not be based on whether I sign this authorization.

9. I understand that information used or disclosed pursuant to this authorization may be disclosed by the recipient and may no longer be protected by federal or state law.

Signature of patient or personal representative: _____

HIPAA Privacy Authorization Form

Authorization for Use or Disclosure of Protected Health Information (Required by the Health Insurance Portability and Accountability Act, 45 C.F.R. Parts 160 and 164)

1. I hereby authorize all medical service sources and health care providers to use and/or disclose the protected health information (PHI) described below to my agent identified in my durable power of attorney for health care named _____

   _____.

2. Authorization for release of PHI covering the period of health care (pick one)

   a. from (date) _____ to (date) _____

   b. All past, present, and future periods.

3. I hereby authorize the release of PHI as follows (pick one):

   a. My complete health record (including records relating to mental health care, communicable diseases, HIV or AIDS, and treatment of alcohol/drug abuse).

   or

   b. My complete health record with the exception of the following information:

   Underline as appropriate:

   Mental health records

   Communicable diseases (including HIV and AIDS)

   Alcohol/drug abuse treatment

   Other (please specify):

   _____ .

4. In addition to the authorization for release of my PHI described in paragraphs 3a and 3b of this authorization, I authorize disclosure of information regarding my billing, condition, treatment, and prognosis to the following individual(s):

   Name: _____ Relationship: _____

   Name: _____ Relationship: _____

   Name: _____ Relationship: _____

5. This medical information may be used by the persons I authorize to receive this information for medical treatment or consultation, billing or claims payment, or other purposes as I may direct.

6. This authorization shall be in force and effect until one year after my death or _____, (date or event) at which time this authorization expires.

7. I understand that I have the right to revoke this authorization, in writing, at any time. I understand that a revocation is not effective to the extent that any person or entity has already acted in reliance on my authorization or if my authorization was obtained as a condition of obtaining insurance coverage and the insurer has a legal right to contest a claim.

8. I understand that my treatment, payment, enrollment, or eligibility for benefits will not be conditioned on whether I sign this authorization.

9. I understand that information used or disclosed pursuant to this authorization may be disclosed by the recipient and may no longer be protected by federal or state law.

Signature:_____

Date: _____

Individual and group plans that provide or pay the cost of medical care are covered entities.

Every health care provider regardless of size who electronically transmits health information in connection with certain transactions is a covered entity. For example. claims, benefit eligibly inquiries

Health care clearinghouses process information they have received from another entity. Health care clearinghouses will receive individually identifiable health information when providing services to a health plan or health care provider. An example of a clearinghouse would be a billing service.

What is personal identifiable health information?

Demographic Information

Demographic data, which relates to:

- The individual's past, present, or future physical or mental health or condition;

- The provision of health care to the individual; or

- The past, present, or future payment for the provision of health care services to the individual. The individual can be identified by name, address, birthdate, social security number, or picture

- The minimum amount of information necessary should be disclosed.

- This does not apply to de-identified information such as when it is redacted (names that are blacked out so individuals cannot be identified).

- Posted in some obvious place there must be a separate description of information such as the information that follows.

Privacy Practice and Notice

- This notice should describe the ways in which the covered entity may use and disclose protected health information.

- The notice must state the covered entity's duties to protect privacy, provide a notice of privacy practices, and the practitioner must abide by the terms of the notice.

- The notice must describe individuals' rights, including the right to complain to Health and Human Services (HHS) and to the covered entity if the person believes his or her privacy rights have been violated.

Covered entities must act in accordance with their notices.

Minors (if the practice includes children)
- In most cases, parents are the personal representatives for their minor children.
- Therefore, parents can exercise individual rights, such as access to the medical record, on behalf of their minor children.
- When the parent is not considered the personal representative, the privacy rule defers to state and/or other laws to clarify the parental rights.

NOTES

Two main types of notes can exist across mental health practices, which include progress notes and psychotherapy notes. There is a clear distinction between the two.

Progress Notes

The basic records detail your client's clinical status during hospitalization or outpatient care. Progress notes are considered part of the client's record. SOAP (subjective, objective, assessment, and plan) notes are a type of progress note tool and include details of your client's symptoms, assessment, diagnosis, and treatment.

The nature of progress notes may vary by state law, federal law and insurance requirements

Psychotherapy Notes

Psychotherapy notes are notes recorded (in any medium) by a mental health professional provider that may include documentation or an analysis of the content of conversation during a private counseling session or a group, joint, or family counseling session that are separated from the rest of the individual's records.

These notes may document conversations you may have had with your client or complex information you might need to recall separately from your progress notes. They can be written in any form useful for you.

Psychotherapy notes exclude (meaning they must be in the progress notes of the record) the following:

1. Medication prescription and monitoring,
2. Counseling session start and stop times

3 Modalities and frequencies of treatment furnished

4 Results of clinical tests

5 Summary of the following items:

- Diagnosis
- Functional status
- The treatment plan
- Symptoms
- Prognosis
- Progress to date

Psychotherapy notes may only be disclosed with authorization (45 C.F.R. § 164.508(a)(2)) except when they are used by the writer of the notes or for a covered entity's supervised mental health education and training purposes.

A health care provider can withhold psychotherapy notes from a patient.

Authorization for release of psychotherapy notes is a specific form of consent. It must include a description of the information to be disclosed, the identity of the person or persons who may disclose the information and to whom it may be disclosed, a description of the purpose of the disclosure, an expiration date for the authorization, and the signature of the person authorizing the disclosure (45 C.F.R. § 164.508(c)).

Below is an example to help illustrate why a patient's mental health records (part of their general health record) are different than psychotherapy notes related to their treatment.

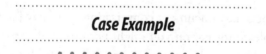

Case Example

Mary is 25 years old and an avid soccer player. She has played since high school and loves the game. One day, Mary begins feeling a sharp pain in her left knee, so she decides she needs to make an appointment with an orthopedic specialist. After seeing Dr. White, he proceeds to document the visit in Mary's general medical record.

The information he includes are the medication he has prescribed for her pain, symptoms, tentative diagnosis of a torn meniscus, and prognosis and any other medical information he thought was important.

Dr. White recommends Mary take a few months off from playing soccer until the pain subsides before they make any decisions about surgery. She follows these recommendations. Over time she notices she is feeling agitated, unmotivated, and is experiencing feelings of hopelessness.

Although Mary has a wide network of friends, she begins to isolate herself and feels depressed. She makes an appointment at her local community health center to see a mental health professional. Mary agrees to have her medical record from Dr. Smith's office released to the clinic.

Mary makes an appointment with a mental health counselor, and after their first meeting the counselor suggests she make an appointment to see the clinic psychiatrist for a consultation. The psychiatrist diagnoses a mild depression and prescribes her medication. The psychiatrist enters this information, along with the start and stop times of the meeting, into Mary's medical record marking it as a mental/behavioral health part of the record, and it becomes a permanent part of Mary's medical record.

The mental health professional has jotted down some notes about her thoughts in relation to Mary. The mental health professional wants to make sure she thinks about some of the information that Mary has discussed and she wants to make sure she heard it accurately, which is why she writes it down. These are considered to be psychotherapy notes and must be kept separate from the medical record. If the therapist includes them in Mary's medical record, they lose their status as psychotherapy notes because they have now become a part of the medical record.

Sometime later, Mary wants a copy of her medical record. She submits a written request for her full medical record to which the clinic responds to and releases Mary's medical record. The information sent to Mary includes everything related to her meniscus treatment and the general and specified information recorded in the mental/behavioral health records.

Mary's therapist has decided that it is not in Mary's best interest to receive this data. Under federal law, this action is a completely compliant and appropriate release by the provider. The therapist also carries no burden to show Mary the psychotherapy notes related to her treatment.

Psychotherapy notes are not immune from inspection. There are instances where you may be required to turn over your psychotherapy notes as required by law, or to comply with any of the following:

1. *A court order or court-ordered warrant, subpoena, or summons issued by a judicial officer*

2. *A grand jury subpoena*

3. *An administrative request from a government agency, including an administrative subpoena or summons, civil or authorized investigative demand, or similar process authorized by law*

Administrative requests sought must be relevant to a legitimate law enforcement inquiry.

GENERAL RECORD KEEPING

The nature and extent of the record will vary depending on the purpose, setting in which the client receives services, and the context of the services. Clinicians must be familiar with legal and ethical requirements for record keeping in their specific jurisdictions. Some states have specific guidelines practitioners must follow, and others do not.

During my internship I was required to take copious and exacting notes. My supervisor wanted a verbatim account of what the client and I had spoken about. The notes were often over fifty pages beginning with sentences such as, "I said, my supervisor said, my patient said. . ." I labored for hours remembering what had occurred. I have since learned that this level of detail is not necessary because records can be entered into court and the content can be hurtful and damaging to clients. If you don't want a client to see information, don't include it in the medical record!

Court proceedings are open to anyone who wants to stop in and listen, except for juvenile court hearings, which are closed to the public.

Case Example

> *You have been working with an individual who has reported years of sexual abuse when she was a child by both her father and grandfather. She has recalled details of the abuse over time. You place the information in her medical record.*
>
> *Your client has become involved in some legal proceeding where her mental state may be at issue. The medical records are called into court.*
>
> *The client's grandfather and father have come to court to support her. If the medical record is filled with details, all that information may be exposed in court. In addition, the accused perpetrators are in court. Certainly there will be legal maneuvering to block the information from being introduced into open court, but the results of the legal argument cannot be determined in advance and the court may order the entire record to be placed into evidence.*
>
> *Previously, I detailed some of the requirements for record keeping under HIPPA laws. If you work in an institution, there are guidelines you must follow. Records can be idiosyncratic for the mental health work you are involved in.*

Nonetheless, I would like to make some general suggestions about the information that you may include in a record. There are three component parts of information to place in a record. Those include identifying information, information for each contact with a client, and other relevant data.

COMPREHENSIVE RECORD INFORMATION

Intake Information

- Basic information on the client, the reasons for referral, and the client's primary concerns. Identifying data (e.g., phone number, address, next of kin, emergency contact, primary care physician)
- Fees and billing information
- Documentation of informed consent or assent for treatment
- Documentation of waivers of confidentiality and consent for release of information
- Documentation of any mandated disclosure of confidential information (e.g., report of child abuse, abuse of the elderly and disabled, danger to self or others, inability to care for one's self by reason of mental illness, secondary to a court order

History

- Personal/family histories, previous interventions or treatments, physical health status

Prior Evaluations and Assessments

- Past and present clinical assessments, previous evaluations, prior testing reports

Diagnoses and Case Formulations

- Plan for services, treatment plan that should be updated as necessary, consultation contacts
- Diagnosis using the DSM-5

Treatment Plan

- Target problems, interventions, reviews, and outcomes
- Other treatment modalities employed, such as medication or biofeedback treatment, EMDR

Progress Notes

- Regular summaries of treatment sessions
- Date of service and duration of session

- Types of services (e.g., consultation, assessment, treatment)
- Current risk factors in relation to dangerousness to self or others

Correspondence

- Records from past treatment providers, notes on all nontrivial phone calls with the client or with other professionals about the client
- Some states may have different laws regarding release of "third party" information. In some states, one can only release records from past or other providers with consent from the client.

Financial Records

- A signed agreement to pay, dates of sessions, charges and payments, and any notes to the client or insurance companies about bills and payments.

Legal Documents

- Any information received or requested from any attorney, (if applicable) including subpoena's, copies of any releases of information for a court matter, guardianship and durable power of attorney paperwork. Anything of a legal matter should be kept in this section.

Termination Summary

- Treatment provided, progress achieved, a prognosis, the reasons for termination, and any clinical recommendations

CHAPTER 6
MENTAL HEALTH IN THE COURTROOM

Mental illness in the courtroom is a complex concept to understand. There is both a psycholegal description of mental illness as well as a psychiatric definition. Depending on the setting, one or both apply. The difference between the two is significant.

In the legal arena decisions are made on issues of competency to stand trial, criminal responsibility, and dangerousness as well as other competencies such as competency to be executed or understanding of Miranda rights.

In the psychiatric arena decisions around differential diagnoses are based on the *Diagnostic and Statistical Manual of Mental Disorders*, Fifth Edition (DSM-5) and/or the *International Classification of Diseases*, Tenth Revision (ICD-10). It is a coding system created in 1989 by the World Health Organization (WHO), which replaced the ICD-9 in 2015.

The DSM-5, the American Psychiatric Association, defines a mental disorder as follows:

"A mental disorder is a syndrome characterized by clinically significant disturbance in an individual's cognition, emotion regulation, or behavior that reflects a dysfunction in the psychological, biological, or developmental processes underlying mental functioning. Mental disorders are usually associated with significant distress in social, occupational, or other important activities. An expectable or culturally approved response to a common stressor or loss, such as the death of a loved one, is not a mental disorder. Socially deviant behavior (e.g., political, religious, or sexual) and conflicts that are primarily between the individual and society are not mental disorders unless the deviance or conflict results from a dysfunction in the individual, as described above."

Statutes generally define mental disorders as:

> *. . . a substantial disorder of thought, mood, perception, orientation or memory that grossly impairs a person's behavior, judgment, capacity to recognize reality, or ability to meet the ordinary demands of life.*

Note that different states use variations of this description. Check your statutes for your state's specificity. In court, the law provides the definition of mental disorder.

COMPETENCE TO STAND TRIAL

Competence to stand trial is a concept of jurisprudence allowing the postponement of criminal proceedings for those defendants who are considered unable to participate in their defense on account of a mental disorder. It is a part of the legal due process guaranteed to us by the US Constitution.

MENTAL CAPACITY

A clinician must confirm that a patient has been told pertinent information directly related to a person's choice concerning the risk and benefits of treatment as well as the prognosis both with and without treatment and about alternative treatments and their risk and benefits as well.

What are the clinical parameters related to the lack of capacity to make treatment decisions in psychiatric patients?

Legal definitions of capacity have shifted from the view as a global, pervasive condition to a more specific condition restricted to particular realms of decision making. This means that diagnostic categories (i.e., schizophrenia) alone cannot decide the issue of decision-making capacity. A person's functional abilities should be considered crucial for mental capacity (i.e., understanding, practical reasoning). A person's capacity should be considered in connection with a particular decision, for example, the capacity to consent to treatment, a voluntary hospitalization, or advance directives, among others.

As mental health practitioners the determination of capacity is our venue. We might assess this skill set by assessing mental status, memory (asking a person to repeat what we have said to them in their own words to determine their understanding) as well as psychological testing, as examples. Competence is defined by the court.

....
Case Example
....

• • • • • • • • • • • •

Joan had been in and out of many psychiatric institutions over a period of ten years. She was a brilliant pianist but her career had been sidetracked because her sole focus encompassed the delusion that Jehovah was coming to earth and would change people's religion to the Jewish faith. Her delusion was entrenched, and no amount of logic would change her thinking. She wandered the hospital floors proselytizing to other patients. Her hospitalizations were brought about because she had been stalking the local priest, calling his home and interrupting his church sermons to state her beliefs.

Joan was admitted to the hospital having been charged with harassment and stalking. When she was in court before the judge rather than replying to the judge's questions, she pontificated. Her attorney was concerned that she would not be able to focus on understanding the various roles and responsibilities of the court personnel or understand the different options in terms of pleadings.

He was also worried that, because of her unremitting focus on her delusion, she would be unable to interact with him and mount a defense to the charges. She consistently spoke over him in conversation. I was tasked with evaluating her skill set as it related to her competency. We had many conversations, some completely based on her belief system while others were coherent and on the point with court proceedings. Although the evaluation took many weeks to complete, I presented my finding to the court when it was complete.

Joan is a woman who has not only significant cognitive limitations but a belief system that interferes with her ability to focus and remain on the topic at hand. However, with prompting and time, it was evident that the skillset for competency were met.

This decision is made solely by the court because it is a legal definition not a psychiatric one. Her capacity was not at issue.

INVOLUNTARY CIVIL COMMITMENT

Involuntary civil commitment is the admission of individuals against their will into a mental health unit. Generally speaking, there are three reasons why an individual with mental illness would be subject to involuntary civil commitment. These include dangerousness to self or others with almost all states construing the inability to provide for one's basic needs as dangerousness to self. Several states incorporate need for treatment. In terms of process, every state provides for a hearing, the right to counsel, and periodic judicial review, while most states have statutory quality standards for treatment and the hospitalization environment.

There must be a nexus between the mental illness and the resulting deficits. The legal standards specifying the criteria for civil commitment and length of time vary widely from state to state. Thus, it is essential to know the civil commitment standards for intervention in your state.

Keep in mind that the presence of a mental illness in and of itself is not a criterion for commitment. Patients with mental illness are guaranteed the same civil liberties as everyone else. Those with schizophrenia who may be calmly wandering the streets talking to themselves have the same right to walk the streets as you or I do.

Hospital dumping has become a euphemism for discharging those with mental illness onto the streets without shelter, money, or medication. Many are encouraged to stay at shelters until they can make suitable living arrangements. Shelters can be dangerous places with theft and violence. Many patients would rather remain on the streets. This is their civil right; we all have the right to be homeless.

Standards of evidence, as described in Chapter 2, for involuntary commitment vary according to state. The majority of states use the clear and convincing standard.

All states have continued to demonstrate the need for close judicial oversight of the commitment process. Given the extensive empirical studies demonstrating the limited reliability of mental diagnoses in legal proceedings, it would certainly be prudent to reevaluate which standard sufficiently protects individuals against wrongful commitments.

Persons subject to involuntary commitment can be emergently deprived of their liberty based on the diagnoses of psychiatrists, emergency room doctors, psychologists, or licensed social workers. Emergency evaluations are often perfunctory. Each state pays particular attention to procedural fairness.

Case Example

You awaken one morning and as you step off the bed you fall. As you struggle to stand up and try to right yourself, you are struck with swirling dizziness and almost lose your balance again. Feeling concerned you call your doctor and make an immediate appointment. You probably shouldn't be driving but because you are in a rush and there is no one else to assist you, you make the decision to do so.

After seeing the doctor, who suspects you might have some sort of inner ear infection, the doctor gives you medication and asks you to sit in the waiting room for twenty minutes to make sure there is no adverse reaction. There is none.

You make your way down the stairs with the intent to get to your car and return home to rest. As you open the door to the outside, the sun blinds you and you suddenly experience severe dizziness. You decide that it may not be wise to drive alone and, having left your phone in the car, your intent is to get it.

Since you are unsteady and worry about falling, you move from object to object holding on and trying desperately to stabilize your balance. You become frightened and to calm yourself you mutter to yourself, "Slowly, carefully, hold on." You notice that your thoughts are becoming increasingly disorganized and find that the sentences flitting through your mind are nonsensical.

Officer Friendly spots you from the Dunkin Donuts where he is having coffee, and comes out to speak with you. You are unsteady, mumbling with disorganized thinking and thus incoherent speech. Your pupils are not dilated nor do you have any odor of alcohol on your breath. What do you think is likely to occur?

My guess is that you will be transported to an emergency room for a psychiatric evaluation in addition to a full physical examination. Any of us can be detained for evaluation and assessment for commitment. Therefore, the standards should meet the highest evidentiary guidelines possible to protect from false positives.

Civil commitment is accomplished based on two theories; parens patriae and the police power of the state

Parens patriae literally means "parent of the country." It provides the sovereign power with authority to protect citizens who, for reasons of mental or physical disability, cannot adequately protect or care for themselves. Intervention by the state is indicated for individuals who are deemed unable to make rational decisions for themselves, including the mentally ill who are "gravely disabled" or suicidal. The state also is obligated to make the decision that is in the best interest of the individual and most clearly reflects the choice that the individual would have made if he or she were competent to do so.

The legal theory of police power provides the state with the authority to act for the protection of society and the general welfare of its citizens. In the process of such protection, isolation and confinement of dangerous individuals, such as those suffering from mental illness, may be necessary because there is a risk to others.

Parens patriae provides for the protection of the individual, and police power generally is invoked on behalf of society against the individual. Having a law does not mean a state makes use of it. Very few states make use of involuntary outpatient commitment, assisted outpatient treatment (AOT) laws.

When inpatient commitment is used, most states rely on the "dangerousness" standard. This standard lacks clarity and is often narrowly interpreted to mean imminently dangerous.

This lack of clarity continues as clinicians struggle with the differentiation between imminent and immediate danger, and if there is any difference at all. The initial finding must be that a person, at the time of clinical evaluation or a court appearance, is a danger to her- or himself or others to be committable.

As previously mentioned, dangerousness is an ambiguous description. It might be understood as the likelihood to intentionally cause serious physical harm to oneself (i.e., suicide) or another (i.e., violence). There are ways to be dangerous to oneself without the intent of harm (or self-mutilation).

Many states have added to their statute grave disability, which is meant to refer to an inability to care adequately for one's own needs even with the assistance of others. In other states, the person must be without basic needs of food, clothing, shelter, or essential medical care.

Can involuntarily hospitalized patients be forced to take medication? Most states consider all patients, even those suffering from a serious mental illness, competent to make personal decisions including whether to take psychotropic medications, unless they are specifically found legally incompetent by a court of law.

Emergency medications, which are contextually different, can be ordered acutely by the treating psychiatrist or a physician for a patient who is considered imminently dangerous to her- or himself or others and refuses to take the medications freely. An example might include a seriously bruised patient suffering from the manic phase of bipolar I who is in restraints but continues to thrash and bangs his face against the bed frame. Emergency medications work for acute situations.

Civil commitment, assessment of dangerousness, and imminent threat are confusing concepts. As long as we apply due diligence, maintain the integrity of patients, keeping in the forefront their vulnerability and care, and follow state statutory guidelines, we are practicing due diligence.

DUTY TO WARN AND LIABILITY

Most states have laws that either require (mandatory) or permit (permissive) mental health professionals to disclose information when they believe patients may pose a risk of imminent danger to themselves or others and protects therapists from both civil and criminal liability for failure to report if they act in good faith.

This area of mental health care, violence, and civil commitment has been recently receiving increased attention in the news following mass shootings, such as James Holmes in Aurora, Colorado; Adam Lanza in Newtown, Connecticut; and Seung-Hui Cho at Virginia Tech, As each was evaluated for dangerousness and later released, the question of prediction of violence and duty to warn has been at the forefront of the media.

With the increased gun violence across the United States there has been attempts to identify, on the basis of mental illness, intellectual developmental disability or other disorder, those who are ineligible to purchase or own a firearm.

Federal law does not require states to submit, despite the ongoing instances of public shootings, to voluntarily report records to National Instant Criminal Background Check System (NCIS). This has produced a slowed process in creating a national database of individuals at risk.

Most states require mental health professionals to report patients likely to harm themselves or others. Illinois has gone a step further and passed the Firearm Concealed Carry Act (PA 98-063), which requires Illinois clinicians to report those they believe pose a "clear and present danger" to themselves or others through the Illinois Firearm Owner's Identification Mental Health Reporting System.

It is likely that other states will follow suit in an attempt to protect the public. However, the difficulty is that the correlation between mental illness and predicting violence is minuscule. This way of thinking ensures maintaining the stigma of mental illness.

Tarasoff v. Regents of University of California. 17 Cal. 3d 425, 131 Cal.Rptr. 14, 551 P.2d 334 (1976) is the case in which the Supreme Court of California decided that mental health professionals have a duty to warn and protect individuals who are being threatened with bodily harm by a patient. The original 1974 decision mandated warning the threatened individual, but on rehearing the case in 1976 the court called for a "duty to protect" the intended victim.

We are all familiar with the fact pattern. Poddar was a student from the untouchable class in India. In September 1967 he entered the University of California, Berkeley, as a graduate student in naval engineering. In the fall of 1968, he attended folk dancing classes where he met 19 year old Tatiana Tarasoff. They saw each other weekly and on New Year's Eve they exchanged a casual kiss. He mistakenly interpreted this action as confirmation of the existence of a serious relationship but Tarasoff was not interested, being in another relationship. Tarasoff who, upon learning of his feelings, explained she was not interested in having an intimate relationship with him. They still interacted occasionally in which Poddar taped the conversations, trying to analyze if she was interested in him. In 1969, Tarasoff traveled to Brazil and Poddar's mental health improved. However, a friend convinced him to go to the counseling center at the university.

The therapist Dr. Moore has been recently traumatized by personal problems. His wife has attempted suicide and attempted to murder their child recently. Nonetheless, Dr. Moore determined that Poddar had an obsession with a young woman who had rejected him, and was fantasizing about harming her. Poddar had seen a psychiatrist previously who diagnosed him with paranoid schizophrenia and prescribed a regimen of medication. From the information Dr. Moore gathered, he determined that he was going to kill a woman on her return. He also had gotten the name. A friend of Poddar had informed Dr. Moore that Poddar had purchased a pellet gun. Dr. Moore requested he turn over the gun, but he did not.

Upon consultation with two other colleagues, they determined that Poddar should be involuntarily committed. Dr. Moore contacted campus police by phone call and letter seeking out a 72-hour evaluation. The police were unclear about the law's application. Poddar denied intent to harm, and she was still in Brazil. He promised to stay away from her. Tatiana Tarasoff's brother, who was Poddar's roommate at the time, was present during the interview. The director of the clinic returned from vacation and, when he found out Poddar had been evaluated, he insisted that Dr. Moore get the letter back and destroy all clinical notes and terminate treatment.

By the time Tarasoff returned, Poddar had moved close to her residence. Two months following his campus police interview, he went to her home with a pellet gun. She refused to see him and he shot her with a pellet gun and chased her with a knife, stabbing her repeatedly.

Poddar was prosecuted for first-degree murder but convicted for second-degree upon testimony by a court-appointed psychiatrist. He was confined to Vacaville State Hospital but was later released by the California Supreme Court due to improper jury instructions. He brokered an agreement not to be retried if he left the country, which he did.

A civil suit was filed by Tarasoff's family. The Supreme Court heard the case twice; one finding was no actual liability admitted by the defendant and on the second hearing established a duty to warn for California.

Because of recently highly publicized and tragic cases such as this, the controversy has also drawn into the public eye the relationship between mental illness and predicting violence.

Published in September 2015, the National Conference of State Legislatures who are tasked with improving the quality and effectiveness of state legislatures and promoting policy innovation and communication among state legislatures developed a list describing each state's laws as they relate to duty to warn. These are summarized below:

State	Duty	Profession
Alabama	Mandatory	Counselors, licensed psychologists, psychiatrists, therapists
Alaska	Permissive	Counselor, psychologist, SW
Arizona	Permissive	Licensed psychologists and support staff
	Mandatory	Behavioral
Arkansas	Permissive	All licensed mental practitioners
California	Mandatory	All licensed mental practitioners
Colorado	Mandatory	All licensed mental practitioners
Conn.	Permissive	Psychologists
Delaware	Mandatory	Mental health service providers
	Permissive	Licensed clinical social workers

State	Duty	Profession
D.C.	Permissive	Mental health professionals
Florida	Permissive	All licensed mental health practitioners
Georgia	No duty	Duty to protect identifiable third parties
Hawaii	Permissive	Psychologists
Idaho	Mandatory	Mental health practitioners
Illinois	Permissive	Therapist
	Mandatory	Physician, psychologist
Indiana	Mandatory	Mental health service providers
Iowa	Mandatory	Mental health service providers
Kansas	Permissive	Undefined
Kentucky	Mandatory	Mental health professionals
Louisiana	Mandatory	Psychologists, psychiatrists, LPC, SW, marriage & family therapists
Maine	No duty	Confidentiality enforced
Maryland	Mandatory	Mental health professional
Mass.	Mandatory	Licensed mental health professionals
Michigan	Mandatory	Mental health professionals
Minn.	Mandatory	Psychologists
Miss.	Permissive	Psychologists, psychiatrists, LPC, SW, marriage & family therapists
Missouri	Mandatory	Mental health coordinators
Montana	Mandatory	Mental health professionals
Nebraska	Mandatory	Psychologists
Nevada	No duty	
N.H.	Mandatory	Licensed psychologists
New Jersey	Mandatory	Psychologists, psychiatrists, MDs, RN, SW marriage counselors
N.M.	Mandatory	Defined by common law
New York	Mandatory	Mental health professionals
N.C.	No duty	
N.D.	No duty	
Ohio	Mandatory	Mental health professionals, services
OK	Permissive	Psychologists, clerical, academic, therapeutic or their employees
Oregon	Permissive	Health care providers
Penn.	Mandatory	Mental health professionals

State	Duty	Profession
R.I.	Permissive	Health care providers
S.C.	Permissive	Mental health professionals
S.D.	Permissive	All record holders
Tenn.	Mandatory	Qualified mental health professional or Behavioral analysts.
Texas	Permissive	Mental health professionals
Utah	Mandatory	Therapist, client must communicate actual threat of violence
Vermont	Mandatory	Mental health agency, psychotherapist, counselor
Virginia	Mandatory	Mental health service providers defined by statute
Wash.	Mandatory	Public, private mental health professionals & agencies
W.V.	Permissive	Mental health professionals
Wisconsin	Mandatory	Psychotherapists
Wyoming	Permissive	Psychologists, professional counselors, marriage & family therapists, SW chemical dependency specialists

I am a firm believer that I am not a detective. It is not my purview to investigate whether a person has made a credible threat. With my best clinical judgment, I complete my assessment. Prior violence, substance abuse, and command hallucinations might increase the risk of violence. The recent research has found that levels of violence are no higher in a control group matched against a group of mentally ill individuals, although the media suggests otherwise.

Nonetheless, the following is a short list of factors you might want to consider in your assessment:

1) What were the events, person's behavior, diagnosis, presence/absence of mental illness/substance abuse, etc.?

2) Who is the potential victim(s)? Some research has shown that if they are violent, individuals with mental illness are more likely to be violent toward family members

3) Is there a plan that includes a date and/or time of the threat?

4) What may be the location and circumstances surrounding the threat?

5 What triggered the violence? Was the violence in retaliation for an imagined or real event? What was the reported motivation behind the behavior? Was it a planned, predatory, or calculated act, or did the violence arise from an emotional trigger in the moment?

6 Is there a pattern in past behaviors? Can this pattern be predicted?

The modern standard in US law was established in *Dusky v. United States* (1960). Although the exact wording varies, all states use a variant of the Dusky standard to define competency (Favole, 1983). In **Dusky v. United States**, 362 U.S. 402 (1960), the Supreme Court held that:

> *Mere presence of severe disturbance (a psychopathological criterion) is only a threshold issue. . .*
>
> *The test of defendant's competency to stand trial is whether he or she has sufficient present ability to consult with his or her lawyer with a reasonable degree of rational understanding and whether he or she has a rational as well as a factual understanding of proceeding against him or her; it is not enough that he or she is oriented to time and place and has some recollection of events. (p. 402)*
>
> *Laws regarding competency vary from state to state, although most jurisdictions follow procedures similar to the overview we will describe in this section. Clinicians should consult their own statute for the specific law and procedure applicable in each state.*
>
> *The issue of competency may be raised at any point in the adjudication process. . .*
>
> *All jurisdictions in the United States provide either statutorily or through case law that information obtained in a competency evaluation cannot be introduced on the issue of guilt unless the defendant places his or her mental state into evidence at either trial or at sentencing hearings*
>
> *A defendant may be psychotic and still be found competent to stand trial if the symptoms do not impair the defendant's functional ability to consult with his or her attorney and otherwise rationally participate in the legal process.*

Civil commitment statutes vary greatly by state in terms of clarity and specificity regarding which mental illnesses are included for the purpose of involuntary hospitalization.

CHAPTER 7

INFORMED CONSENT

No matter which discipline you have been trained in, the issue of informed consent has been at the forefront of your work in mental health care. It has both legal and ethical significance. In general terms, informed consent is the articulation of a person's preferences and their right to make autonomous decisions in a variety of areas of their lives.

Informed consent occurs in the context of the therapeutic relationships, fiduciary relationships, right to choose care and what kind of care to choose, and the right to participate in research, or to decline care, to name a few examples. It is a person's right to understand and exercise these rights freely.

Informed consent has been generally conceptualized as having three core components: understanding of information, decision-making capacity, and voluntariness.

In a court of law if a respondent pleads guilty, a judge will address questions to the respondent in what might best be described as a colloquy. The initial question is to verify that an individual who pleads guilty and surrenders his or her right to a trial in making a plea understands the first component of informed consent.

The next question addresses whether the person is able to make a decision and not having his or her cognition affected by any substance that might affect the ability to weigh the advantages and disadvantages of that person's decision.

The final question is to make certain that the person has independently made the decision without undue influence from another person.

In mental health the importance of informed consent arose out of a number of arenas. The first chapter of this book addressed some situations where independent decisions were not taken into consideration. Individuals who are severely mentally ill are often considered incapable of giving informed consent without a court decision. As I have mentioned previously, you should always assume competence unless a court determines otherwise.

The issue of informed consent grew in large part out of the fear that clinicians were negligent in advising clients of their treatment options available to choose in the marketplace. In the twenty-first century treatment options for patients have become of utmost importance since new treatment modalities are developing at a rapid pace.

For example, eye movement desensitization and reprocessing (EMDR) therapy, developed by Dr. Francine Shapiro in 1985, is a psychotherapy approach that has been extensively researched and proven effective for the treatment of trauma.

Dr. Marsha Linehan's model of dialectical behavior therapy (DBT), developed in the 1970s, is a cognitive-behavioral treatment developed to treat chronically suicidal individuals diagnosed with borderline personality disorder (BPD). It is now recognized as the gold standard treatment for this population. Further research has shown that it can also be effective in treating other disorders such as substance dependence, depression, post-traumatic stress disorder (PTSD), and eating disorders.

Brainspotting (BSP), a modified version of EMDR, was developed by Dr. David Grand in 2003. As a newer type of therapy it was designed to help people access, process, and overcome trauma, negative emotions, and pain, including psychologically induced physical pain. Trained BSP therapists guide the eyes of people in therapy across their field of vision to find a brainspot, which is an eye position that activates a traumatic memory or painful emotion. Practitioners trained in this procedure believe it allows therapists to access emotions on a deeper level as well as target the physical effects of trauma. The theory is based on the increasing evidence that trauma is "stored" in the body and that it can alter the way the brain works. Trauma can have an effect on emotions, memory, and physical health. Brainspotting is believed to activate the body's inherent ability to heal itself from trauma.

As is familiar to all of us, the practice of medicine for centuries has followed the Hippocratic oath with emphasis on protecting the patient from harm. In the mid-twentieth century the rights of patients began to appear in legal cases against physicians.

In *Canterbury v. Spence*, 464 F.2d 772 (D.C. Cir. 1972), Canterbury (the plaintiff) had surgery on his back conducted by Dr. Spence (the defendant). Spence did not tell Canterbury of the possible risks of the surgery. While performing the surgery Dr. Spence found that there was swelling on the patient's spinal cord and conducted a procedure to relieve the pressure. During recovery the patient slipped and was almost rendered paralyzed.

Canterbury sued Dr. Spence on the grounds that Dr. Spence did not inform him of the potential risks of the surgery. Barring the complex legal history, the issue the court decided to consider was the question as to whether a physician should inform a patient of all reasonable risks involved with the proposed treatment? If you had had either major or minor surgery, the answer would be a resounding yes.

In mental health law, ***Osherhoff v. Chestnut Lodge***, 490 A.2d 72 (Md. App. 1985), is viewed as the landmark case for informed consent to psychotherapy. Dr. Osheroff was hospitalized for a year at Chestnut Lodge for depression. After undergoing a year of extensive but unsuccessful psychoanalysis as the form of treatment, Dr. Osheroff discontinued therapy. After seeing a psychopharmacologist he began a course of antidepressant medications to which he reportedly responded well.

In this case, Dr. Osheroff claimed negligence asserting that he had not been told of the option to take medicine to treat depression. He further claimed that had he known of this option he would have been spared a year of severe psychological distress plus the financial burden. This case was settled out of court, but it was powerful in shifting attention to the role of informed consent in psychotherapy. It is each therapist's duty to present clear information in relation to the nature and goals of treatment and goals of therapy and viable treatment alternatives. This notable case brought about the formalization of ethical standards that require informed consent to therapy.

Taking the finding of this case a bit further, it also addresses concerns we, as practitioners, might face when we treat a client with an unsuccessful or unconventional modality.

For example, I saw a client who was suffering from a persistent intractable depression. We worked together for six months with little improvement. After discussion and analysis of other possible modalities of treatment, which we had discussed early on, I facilitated a referral for cognitive-behavioral treatment.

Clients often have erroneous and magical ideas about what therapy can help them attain. It is not uncommon for clients to expect results in a short period of time. Informed consent also sets the framework for a balanced and healthy relationship and realistic expectations. It highlights the patient's role in decision making.

Informed consent to psychotherapy not only satisfies the ethics of professional practice but serves as a framework for a balanced and healthy relationship. The information must fit each client's strengths and vulnerabilities. There is a difference in how we might present this information to a patient who is actively experiencing auditory hallucinations or someone who has cognitive limitations.

BOUNDARIES

Boundaries in the context of psychotherapy explain the parameters of the therapeutic relationship as well as the fiduciary responsibilities in its undertaking. A therapeutic relationship is different from a social, friendship, intimate, sexual, or business relationship. The therapeutic setting presents some unique qualities in these relationships around self-disclosure, physical contact, both receiving and giving gifts, and visits outside the usual office site where therapy takes place, to name a few.

Sexual misconduct with clients is not a new subject. There are reports of sexual misconduct and abuse by some of the pioneering theorists of the nineteenth and twentieth century.

Psychoanalyst Carl Jung had a romantic relationship with Sabina Spielrein, whom he treated from 1905 to 1909. She was 19 years old when she began her analysis. There were reports of correspondence between Jung and Freud concerning this relationship until their split as cohorts in 1913.

Biographers report that Karen Horney, who gave birth to the notion that neurotic feelings and attitudes are determined by the way we live versus Freud's ideas that instinctual drives are biologically determined, allegedly became sexually involved with patients and students with some regularity.

Frieda Fromm-Reichmann, an innovator of applying psychoanalysis for the treatment of schizophrenia, acknowledged engaging in a romantic relationship with a patient, her future husband, Erich Fromm who was one of her analysands (a person undergoing psychoanalysis). According to one author Fromm-Reichmann congratulated herself for having the "common sense" to end the therapist/patient relationship before they married.

Bruno Bettelheim maintained an international reputation for his work on psychoanalysis, autistic children, and child rearing. As director of the Orthogenic School, Bettelheim created an environment in which to care for children entrusted to him. Former students accused him of creating an atmosphere of terror in the school including emotional and physical brutality and sexual abuse. He has been accused of plagiarism, falsifying his credentials, and shoddy research.

Therapist malpractice insurance policies frequently include clauses providing that the insurance company is not liable for claims arising from the therapist's sexual misconduct.

Boundary violations are actions by a practitioner that are harmful, exploitative, or in direct conflict with the dignity of a client. Under the law, the action has had to cause serious harm for which a civil court can provide a remedy.

However, even if such issues do not result in legal action against a therapist, they are frequently the cause of complaints to ethics committees or licensure boards.

The atmosphere of therapy has changed. It is not unusual for adolescents to request a meeting at a local coffee shop, like Dunkin Donuts, as if the donuts will facilitate conversation. When we work with children, it is not uncommon for them, when they become familiar with a therapist, to issue a greeting with a big hug. In recent times, the physical contact between a patient and a therapist may result in grave consequences if it is misunderstood.

When clinicians depart from a traditional constraint, or therapy setting, that is intended to and beneficial to a client, there is a risk involved.

Prohibited dual relationships are always unethical, but there are some boundary crossings that are not unethical. The problem with boundary crossings is that they increase the risk of the so-called "slippery slope" phenomenon.

Here are some basic suggested guidelines for therapists when responding to a patient's request to step outside of the traditional therapeutic framework:

1. Ask yourself how the patient's request can be addressed within a traditional therapeutic framework.

2. Consider the ways in which the request may reflect a desire on the part of the patient for the therapist to meet the needs of the patient, which were unmet by important people in the patient's life.

3. Interpret (rather than gratify) the request whenever appropriate.

4. Is your response culturally appropriate?

5. Always consult with a colleague before stepping outside traditional therapeutic boundaries.

If you are seeking legal advice, do not consult with a colleague, call a lawyer. Many of the professional organizations, state association's licensing boards, and malpractice insurers have lawyers on staff. You can consult with one of these individuals in relation to your general questions.

If you have questions about the laws in the state in which you practice, it is important to consult with someone who knows the laws in that particular state.

Think about the following situations and how you might manage them, keeping risk in mind.

·············
Case Example
·············

• • • • • • • • • • •

A man comes to you who states that he is in an unhappy marriage. He reports that he has been trying for years to work out compromises in the relationship but has not been successful. He feels that at this juncture he is so unhappy that he wants to dissolve the marriage. Matters have been complicated because as a last resort, the couple had a baby hoping it would repair the damage and give the couple a new start. It didn't work.

You have never seen the biological mother. The divorce process is acrimonious and all decision making in relation to custody and visitation is decided by the court. This makes suggestions about changing arrangements financially costly.

Your client meets someone new and after a courtship remarries. The biological mother is furious and requests that the new stepmother does not come with him to pick up and drop off their daughter. She has demanded that the stepmother be dropped off at a nearby mall when the transfer occurs so they need not meet.

Needless to say the request produces conflict within the couple. Your patient requests that you begin to see them in couple's therapy additionally to help them negotiate this dilemma. He wants to continue individually to discuss his own issues.

In addition, your client's new wife has been looking for a therapist and reports to you she has met many practitioners but feels you are the best to meet her needs and inquires as to whether you would meet with her individually as well.

Decision-Making Thoughts

- To whom do you owe confidentiality?

- What are the risks of seeing all involved simultaneously?

- How many records do you have if you decide to proceed?

- Does confidentiality exist for information shared by each of the parties?

- Are you able to keep the information separate in your mind?

Most practitioners would elect not to work with more than one client and refer the couple and the wife to different therapists. However, if you practice using a family systems approach, the theory suggests that individuals cannot be understood in isolation from one another, but they are part of a family, which is the emotional unit.

There are unusual guidelines that apply to couples therapy. Perhaps as the clinician you might meet with each member of the couple once or twice to get a sense of their perspective on their goals. Explain to them that nothing shared is confidential from the other so there will be no secrets.

For example, one partner comes into therapy and says, "Doctor, I am having an incredible affair with this person I have met. It is the best sex I have ever had. If I would have known what was possible I would never have married my husband, he is a dud." Hopefully, you would choose not to take this information back to the couple and become a conduit by addressing Mr. Dud.

Case Example

Your client has invited you and your significant other to their wedding.

Decision-Making Thoughts

- What is the meaning of the invitation?
- Who will your client want you to identify yourself as?
- Do you attend both the ceremony and the reception?
- Do you bring your significant other?

- Do you bring a gift? What kind? How much should you spend?
- Do you expect your client to pay for your time? If so, how do you determine a rate?
- You don't want to go, how do you handle that?

Case Example

Your client has voiced how grateful he is to you and has given you a gift that appears expensive.

Decision-Making Thoughts

- Do you accept it?
- You may lean forward in your chair towards your client and say to the client, "Do you ask how much it was?" That would certainly have destructive consequences.
- What does giving a gift mean to the client?
- How would your client interpret a refusal?
- How might you show your gratitude?

When you look on the Internet for guidance on these situations, the information found largely suggests acceptance produces harmful effects: issues of buying love, warning signs of questionable therapy, retraumatization of a client.

I had a client whom I worked with for over ten years. Since she was an animal lover and committed to the caring of animals, I had shared with her that I had two dogs as a means to connect with her early on.

From that day forward, once a month she would bring two rawhide treats for my dogs. I never refused (which I believe made my dogs joyous) to accept them. We talked about the meaning of the gesture for her and what her intention was. In my opinion, it was therapeutic for her to do this, which satisfied my professional ethical guidelines.

Context and culture are equally important. In some cultures it would be considered disrespectful to decline a gift. Still, some agencies have policies about accepting gifts.

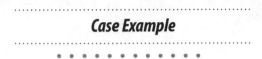

Case Example

*You are an active member in a religious institution or
large organization and a client seeks out your services.*

Decision-Making Thoughts

- What is the extent of your involvement in the organization?
- How large is the organization?
- Have you discussed how your client will feel seeing you regularly outside of your office?
- What if your family members accompany you to the setting?

These are all things we should be considering. The world can be a small place. These are questions that are also particularly applicable if you practice in a small or isolated community. What if you're the only practitioner for those who live a great distance from a city. Or, you practice in a defined community such as a college counseling center, where you might attend campus events.

Case Example

A client wants to barter for your services.

Decision-Making Thoughts

- Is it culturally appropriate?
- Is this form of payment suitable for you in terms of your livelihood?
- Is there another meaning for your client with this arrangement?
- How do you agree on a fair price for number of sessions?

Case Example

Your client loses her job and subsequently loses her health insurance. The search for another job has not yet been successful.

Decision-Making Thoughts

• Do you scale your fees?

If you choose to scale payment for your services, make certain the guideline are clearly stated in your informed consent.

Case Example

A client wants to hug you every time they come to a session.

Decision-Making Thoughts

• How could your client interpret physical contact?
• What is enough and when is it too much?
• How do you discuss the issue with your client?

If you choose to be a nontouching therapist, inform your clients in the informed consent that you will not engage in physical contact with them. Make sure whatever you do is documented.

CHAPTER 8
PRIVILEGED COMMUNICATION

In *Jaffee v. Redmond,* 135 L. Ed. 2d 337 (S. Ct. 1996), the US Supreme Court looked at the parameters of privilege for psychotherapeutic communications in the federal courts. The US Supreme Court made it clear that confidentiality in psychotherapy takes singular precedence. HIPAA's protection for medical privacy rule by the Department of Health and Human Services relied on this case in providing additional legal protections for confidential psychotherapy.

The defendant, Mary Redmond, a police officer, shot and killed Ricky Allen to prevent what she believed was going to be the stabbing of an innocent victim. The Allen family brought suit against the officer alleging unconstitutional use of force because there seemed to be conflicts around Redmond's recall of the event. Officer Redmond sought counseling from a licensed clinical social worker and had approximately fifty counseling sessions. Allen's family sought to get the records of the counseling sessions. Officer Redmond refused, citing psychotherapist-patient privilege. The family sought monetary damages for wrongful death. Redmond would not comply.

The lower trial court found that the federal rules did not provide for a psychotherapist-patient privilege. The US Supreme Court agreed to review the lower court's denial of such a privilege, finding that confidential communications of a police officer with a licensed social worker were protected from compelled disclosure.

Effective psychotherapy depends on an atmosphere of confidence/trust in which a patient is willing to make complete disclosure of facts, emotions, memories, and fears, and this right serves important private and public interests. The mental health of the citizenry is a public good of great importance.

The right to privacy refers to the broad principle that one's personal information is protected from public scrutiny. It is essentially the right to be left alone.

The right to privacy most often is protected by federal law. For example, HIPAA protects a person's health information.

In determining laws relating to the right to privacy of citizens, court decisions are balanced against the state's compelling interests such as the promotion of public safety and improving the quality of life. An example would be the laws regarding the use of seat belts.

The right to privacy means the right to personal autonomy, or the right to choose whether or not to engage in certain acts. The right to privacy is most often cited in the Due Process Clause of the Fourteenth Amendment, which states:

> *No state shall make or enforce any law which shall abridge the privileges or immunities of citizens of the United States; nor shall any state deprive any person of life, liberty, or property, without due process of law; nor deny to any person within its jurisdiction the equal protection of the laws.*

Confidentiality refers to the ethical duty of a licensed clinician not to disclose information learned from the patient to any other person or organization without the consent of the patient.

A duty is a legal obligation owed to a person to which another person has a corresponding legal right. In the case of the psychotherapist-patient legal relationship, confidentiality is the duty not to disclose certain information without proper authorization leaves practitioners open to civil liability. Confidentiality applies in other instances as well.

A therapist was conducting group therapy with eight individuals. He was also a professor in one of the universities teaching the same subject matter. While the group was meeting one evening, one of the patients looked at a piece of paper resting on a file cabinet. It was a complete description of her, her concerns and a verbatim report of conversations from the group. Although no names were used, the description was so complete that she feared she might be identified. She sued the psychotherapist for breach of confidentiality and won a tidy sum.

If there are activities you, as a licensed therapist, routinely participate in and you wish to use client information, you must request and receive consent. Many of us are members of collegial support or supervision groups where confidential client information may be discussed. If this is the case, get written consent from each person. If a person fails to give consent, then you must protect not only that person's name but all the information he or she has spoken about in the context of psychotherapy. Failure to do so leaves the door open for a civil suit against you.

Privilege, a legal right, usually takes the form of an exemption from the duty to do something. In clinical work, the way this most often takes form is as an exemption from a duty to provide information in a legal proceeding.

The circumstances in which confidentiality can be breached are defined by state and federal case law, or both.

THIRD-PARTY REIMBURSEMENT

Each insurance or managed care company has its own criteria for authorizing sessions. By seeking reimbursement from a third party payer, the therapist may be required to provide information about diagnosis and treatment to the company that administers the third-party reimbursement. Insurers can submit medical data to national data banks where the material then becomes accessible to other insurers and, potentially, to other parties.

The rules of confidentiality about how insurance and managed care companies record and use information provided to them may not conform to the customary and usual therapeutic norms of confidentiality. Information contained in medical records maintained by third-party providers may sometimes have possible implications for future employment, future insurance, security clearances, child custody, and other legal involvements.

COLLECTION OF DEBT

If in your informed consent you notify a client that you reserve the right to utilize the services of a debt collection agency or small claims court in the event payment is in arrears, once you have received the consent of a client, you are free to use these avenues. In my opinion, however, the use of collection agencies is not a feasible path for many reasons.

First, once the practitioner turns over the debt owed to an agency the practitioner has little control over what kind of practices these agencies employ. Some use harassing phone calls, embarrassing calls to family members and employers, and all kind of threats. Not unlike mortgages, it can also be sold to third parties for collection. The use of a collection agency may negatively impact a clients' credit rating.

It is not uncommon for the party owed not to receive an adequate return of the debt owned. Most of the debt goes uncollected and the remainder owed goes to the collection agency.

The risk is that the attempts to collect unpaid bills can lead clients to file complaints with the licensing boards or to file malpractice suits. The charges in such filings do not center on the debt but on substandard care and/or harm caused by the therapists. Even unfounded board complaints can result in an investigation.

In this digital age, it may only take one person to post a scathing review on Yelp or other sites to cause significant harm to a therapist's reputation, referrals, and practice in general. However, if you do elect to utilize this path, the client has agreed to only release the information necessary to institute the collection process, not their entire confidential record.

DEFENSE OF MALPRACTICE OR PROFESSIONAL COMPLAINTS

Many states have not enacted laws regarding exceptions to privilege. It is important for you to check your particular state law. In relation to malpractice actions, accused therapists must have the ability to defend themselves against a civil malpractice action brought by a client in relation to any part of their work together. Therefore, these actions serve as an exception to the rules of privilege. Dr. Gerald P. Koocher, past president of the American Psychological Association among other roles, and versatile teacher at many universities, suggests that licensing boards or professional association ethics committees have no avenue to investigate a complaint against a mental health practitioner unless the complainant waives the duty of confidentiality.

Safety parameters have been set in place by most ethics committees. Generally, all proceedings are conducted in confidential sessions and assure privacy to complainants. In malpractice cases, judges can order spectators excluded from the courtroom and place records related to sensitive testimony under seal from the public's view.

THE PATRIOT ACT OF 2001

After the events of September 11, 2001, Congress passed the USA PATRIOT Act. The purpose of the legislation is to make it easier for law enforcement to act to prevent future acts of terrorism. This PATRIOT Act authorizes certain FBI agents to request a subpoena from a special court. The FBI can require access to any requested records, and the subject of the investigation (i.e., the patient) may not be notified. In fact, telling clients their clinical records have been subpoenaed by the FBI is not permitted and can result in serious penalties. In 2006 an addendum was added to the law that includes the requirement that requested records are identified as pertinent to the activities of a suspected terrorist or person in contact with a suspected terrorist.

CONFIDENTIALITY AND HIV

HIV carries with it a unique stigma that affects nearly every aspect of a client's life. Depending on the area of the country where you practice, public knowledge, and awareness, there may be a unique stigma that can insidiously affect different aspects of a person's life. Some may choose to keep their diagnosis a secret, hidden from employers, coworkers, neighbors, family, and friends, while others are unconcerned.

Clients with HIV are like other clients with a serious illness. Twenty years ago such a diagnosis would follow a course toward death. With advances in treatment, HIV is now a chronic illness.

The issue of a client with HIV or AIDS engaging in unprotected sex with other individuals who are unaware produces serious concerns. Knowledge of this behavior understandably produces visceral responses from practitioners. None of us want to see another person placed in harm's way.

With regard to breaching confidentiality, there are several relevant issues. These include: intent to do harm, likelihood of actual harm occurring, the inability to know the identity of future sexual partners, and two adults consensually engaging in these behaviors. When it comes to unprotected sexual behavior, one might reasonably argue that your client's partners are engaging in this behavior consensually.

Is this a duty to warn/protect issue in those states where this is statutorily or case law defined? Is there an unwitting partner who may become infected? In some states, such as Illinois, only physicians can reveal this information, and only under certain circumstances.

It is important to know the requirements of your state's laws. Some states do not require the reporting of HIV or AIDS status by licensed psychotherapists while other states do require reporting. Knowledge of the relevant laws in one's jurisdiction is essential. It is also important to keep in mind that breaching confidentiality due to harm to others has strict limitations. The harm must be threats of harm in the future, not in the past or ongoing. This also leaves the question as to whether it is outside the boundaries of our competence as non-physicians to warn of a medical diagnosis.

There has been a wealth of education about sexually transmitted diseases, practicing safe sex, methods of transmission, and risks involved. In considering the lethality of someone's actions, unprotected sex by an HIV-positive or AIDS-infected individual does not possess the lethality of shooting or stabbing. Additionally, the chances of becoming infected during unprotected sex is not absolute. In this instance it is not only important to document your actions but the thinking behind them.

·············
Case Example
·············
· · · · · · · · · · · ·

> *Lance comes to you for therapy. He is engaged to be married in the spring. He brings his fiancée with him one day so they can talk about the upcoming wedding and for you to meet her. You notice he is sullen in her presence.*
>
> *Over the course of a few months he tells you he is HIV positive and is struggling whether to tell his fiancée, since he has not done so. He is visibly upset and struggling. The wedding is approaching.*
>
> *He has been reluctant to tell you whether they are having safe sex so you are not certain. What are your legal and ethical responsibilities?*

DOMESTIC VIOLENCE

Treatment programs have previously been designed solely for men becoming violent with an intimate partner. Many men have been court mandated to attend what has euphemistically been called anger management groups. These groups were primarily focused on education, which over the long run has not been proven as the most effective intervention. Many defendants who have been ordered to attend these groups refer to them as ineffective. The literature also suggests that individuals who have a problem with violence sometimes suffer from psychiatric symptoms as well. With the recent changes in domestic violence laws, alternative programs have proliferated. At the forefront, of course, is the safety of participants and that nexus with confidentiality.

It is important to clarify the kind of treatment you are offering. Educational approaches essentially do not meet the requirements to keep a patient record. The location of where the class is conducted also communicates information. If held in a clinic environment, the perception might be that the group is psychotherapy. Clarity about the nature of the services being offered should be articulated in your informed consent.

Other important questions to think about have to do with specific state-mandated and disclosure laws particularly as they include children in the environment. The question needing to be addressed is who could also suffer harm and should be warned. This could include children, roommates, and other family members whom the offender had previously threatened or actually assaulted, or those in close proximity to the potential victim. Some states have language in their child abuse reporting laws indicating that a child witnessing abuse is reportable.

There also may be more situations where there is no specific threat made by the client, but nevertheless, there still exists a duty to protect the client from harming him- or herself or others. Therefore, therapists working with perpetrators of domestic violence must carefully assess their client's potential of risk for harm and set up parameters within their program or treatment.

In those states that require either mandated or permissive duty to warn, information disclosed to a mental health provider that is either an explicit threat of serious harm or death to clearly identified victims displaying intent and ability to carry out the threat, laws of confidentiality are trumped and must be reported as specified in state statute.

CHILD PORNOGRAPHY, CONFIDENTIALITY, AND MANDATED REPORTING

The issue of downloading child pornography from the Internet and other child pornography activities have been controversial recently. The federal mandatory minimum sentences for sex crimes against children are strict: five years for downloading pornography, fifteen years for producing it, and thirty years for sex with a victim who is under 16 and at least four years younger than the perpetrator.

So far, California is the only state that has made state law around this issue. Effective January 1, 2015, California Penal Code section 11165 was amended to require psychotherapists to report their clients if the psychotherapist learns that the client is downloading, streaming, or accessing child pornography.

This bill defines sexual exploitation as a person who with knowledge downloads, streams, or accesses through any electronic or digital media, film, photograph, videotape, video recording, or slide in which a child is engaged in an act of obscene sexual conduct.

Using the model of addiction, consider you have a patient who reports he has had sexual contact with a sibling in the past. During the treatment he says that he is reluctant to tell his partner of the abuse for fear she may think he will abuse their children. Another example might concern a patient who discloses his sexual feelings, possession of child pornography, and subsequent fantasies of behaviors related to children.

What about visual depictions that include photographs, videos, digital or computer-generated images indistinguishable from an actual minor, and images created, adapted, or modified but appear to depict an identifiable, actual minor; undeveloped film, undeveloped videotape, and electronically stored data that can be converted into a visual image of child pornography?

There are many questions to contemplate. In recent years, as can be seen in California, there has been a massive effort to identify who these individuals may be and not only the extent of the obsession but whether or not the information we have rises to the level requiring mandated reporting. As you think about your legal and ethical responsibilities, keep in mind that you are not law enforcement. Our duty is only to report, not to investigate whether an action actually occurred or whether it is a punishable offense.

Case Example

• • • • • • • • • • •

Ron, who works in a court setting, has been referred to you by the court psychologist. This is not court-mandated treatment. He is anxious in the first couple of meetings. He has been married for a year and he and his wife are contemplating having a child in the near future.

Ron then tells you that he has been viewing pornography involving minor children and finds this almost uncontrollably arousing. He says he is a member of one of the websites where members can communicate with each other and share films. He tells you that when he has sex with his wife, in order to get aroused, he fantasizes about children.

Ron is struggling with trying to figure out if he may be a pedophile. He tells you that when he was a young boy, he had several sexual exploration experiences with other young boys in his neighborhood. He reports that he has never touched a child inappropriately but wonders about his ability to maintain control of these urges.

What are your legal and ethical responsibilities?

Do those change if instead Ron is Ronnie, a woman?

WHAT IS CHILD ABUSE?

Child abuse is when a parent or caregiver, whether through action or failing to act, causes injury, death, emotional harm, or risk of serious harm to a child. There are many forms of child maltreatment, including neglect, physical abuse, sexual abuse, exploitation, and emotional abuse.

Physical abuse of a child is when a caregiver causes any nonaccidental physical injury to a child. Sexual abuse occurs when an adult uses a child for sexual purposes or involves a child in sexual acts. It also includes when a child who is older or more powerful uses another child for sexual gratification or excitement.

When a parent or caregiver harms a child's mental and social development or causes severe emotional harm, this is child abuse. While a single incident may be considered abuse, most identify child abuse as a pattern of this behavior over time.

Child neglect is when the caregiver does not give the care, supervision, affection, and support needed for a child's health, safety and well-being. Neglect includes: physical neglect, emotional neglect, and medical neglect.

- How is child abuse and neglect defined in your state law? Does your state define a child witnessing domestic violence as a form of abuse or neglect?

- Federal legislation lays the groundwork for state laws on child maltreatment by identifying a minimum set of acts or behaviors that define child abuse and neglect. The federal Child Abuse Prevention and Treatment Act (CAPTA), 42 U.S.C.A. §5106g, as amended and reauthorized by the CAPTA Reauthorization Act of 2010, defines child abuse and neglect as, at minimum:

Any recent act or failure to act on the part of a parent or caretaker which results in death, serious physical or emotional harm, sexual abuse or exploitation; or an act or failure to act which presents an imminent risk of serious harm.

Mandatory Reporting

Some professionals are required by law to report suspected child abuse and neglect. It may be a misdemeanor for a mandated reporter to fail to report suspected child abuse or neglect or knowingly make a false report, and it is punishable under law.

If a mandatory reporter has:

> A reasonable belief to suspect that a child has been subjected to abuse or neglect or has directly observed a child being subjected to conditions that would reasonably result in abuse or neglect.

Risk Factors for Child Abuse and Neglect

While child abuse and neglect occurs in all types of families—even in those that look happy from the outside—children are at a much greater risk in certain situations.

1. **Domestic violence.** Witnessing domestic violence is terrifying to children and emotionally abusive. Even if the mother does her best to protect her children and keeps them from being physically abused, the situation is still extremely damaging. If you or a loved one is in an abusive relationship, getting out is the best thing for protecting the children.

2. **Alcohol and drug abuse.** Living with an alcoholic or addict is very difficult for children and can easily lead to abuse and neglect. Parents who are drunk or high are unable to care for their children, make good parenting decisions, and control often-dangerous impulses. Substance abuse also commonly leads to physical abuse.

3. **Untreated mental illness.** Parents who suffer from depression, an anxiety disorder, bipolar disorder, or another mental illness have trouble taking care of themselves, much less their children. A mentally ill or traumatized parent may be distant and withdrawn from his or her children, or quick to anger without understanding why. Treatment for the caregiver means better care for the children.

4. **Lack of parenting skills.** Some caregivers never learned the skills necessary for good parenting. Teen parents, for example, might have unrealistic expectations about how much care babies and small children need. Or parents who were themselves victims of child abuse may only know how to raise their children the way they were raised. In such cases, parenting classes, therapy, and caregiver support groups are great resources for learning better parenting skills.

5. **Stress and lack of support.** Parenting can be a very time-intensive, difficult job, especially if you're raising children without support from family, friends, or the community or you're dealing with relationship

problems or financial difficulties. Caring for a child with a disability, special needs, or difficult behaviors is also a challenge. It's important to get the support you need, so you are emotionally and physically able to support your child.

ELDER ABUSE

Case Example

. . . .

Ann's elderly mother is welcomed into her family, which consists of her husband and her two teenage sons who are still a handful. Ann works part time but her husband works from their home and is home with Ann's mother during the day. The two agree that he will be responsible for her care during the day and Ann will take over when she returns from work.

It seems to be working out well for a few months, but Ann notices changes in her mother's physical well-being. Her mother's clothes are often dirty, and when Ann has taken sheets off her mother's bed she notices there is dried feces on the sheets. As time goes on Ann has come home early on several occasions and found her mother still in bed. Her mother consistently has food crust on her face. She asks her husband about these changes and he gets annoyed telling her is doing the best he can.

Elder abuse is the infliction of physical, emotional/psychological, sexual, or financial harm on an older adult. Elder abuse can also take the form of intentional or unintentional neglect of an older adult by the caregiver.

Physical abuse can range from slapping or shoving to severe beatings and restraining with ropes or chains. When a caregiver or other person uses enough force to cause unnecessary pain or injury, even if the reason is trying to help the older person, the behavior can be regarded as abusive. Physical abuse can include hitting, beating, pushing, shoving, kicking, pinching, burning, or biting. It also includes the inappropriate use of medications and physical restraints and physical punishment of any kind.

Verbal, emotional or psychological abuse can range from name calling or giving the silent treatment to intimidating and threatening the individual.

When a family member, a caregiver, or another person behaves in a way that causes fear, mental anguish, or emotional pain or distress, the behavior can be regarded as abusive. Verbal and emotional abuse can include yelling, swearing, and making insulting or disrespectful comments. Psychological abuse involves any type of coercive or threatening behavior that sets up a power differential between the older adult and his or her family member or caregiver. It can also include treating the older person like a child and isolating the person from family, friends, and regular activities through force, threats, or manipulative behavior.

Sexual abuse can range from sexual exhibition to rape. Sexual abuse can include inappropriate touching, photographing the person in suggestive poses, forcing the person to look at pornography, forcing sexual contact with a third party, or any unwanted sexualized behavior. It also includes rape, sodomy or coerced nudity. Sexual abuse is perhaps the most egregious but least reported type of elder abuse.

Financial abuse and exploitation can range from misuse of an older person's funds to embezzlement. Financial exploitation includes fraud, taking money under false pretenses, forgery, forced property transfers, purchasing expensive items with the older person's money without that person's knowledge or permission, or denying the older person access to his or her own funds or home. It includes the improper use of legal guardianship arrangements, powers of attorney, or conservatorships. It also includes a variety of Internet, telephone, and face-to-face scams perpetrated by salespeople—or even by so-called friends—for health-related services, home repair services, mortgage companies, and financial services.

Caregiver neglect can range from caregiving strategies that withhold appropriate attention from the individual to intentionally failing to meet the physical, social, or emotional needs of the older person. Neglect can include failure to provide food, water, clothing, medications, and assistance with activities of daily living or help with personal hygiene. If the caregiver is responsible for paying bills for the older person, neglect can also include failure to pay the bills or to manage the older person's money responsibly. Family caregivers may inadvertently neglect their older relatives because of their own lack of knowledge, resources, or maturity, although this is a less frequent form of abuse.

Case Example

• • • • • • • • • • •

Madeline is 70 and suffers from congestive heart failure. She lives alone and home health nurses and nurses' aides come in daily to provide nursing care and personal assistance. She depends on the home health agency's personal assistant to help her with the routine tasks around the house and to provide interaction with someone from the outside world. At first, the assistant was sweet to Madeline, but lately, the assistant has started ignoring Madeline's requests, snapping at her, and bumping into her with the vacuum cleaner or dusting brush while cleaning. Madeline thinks the assistant is bumping her on purpose, but she does not know for sure, and she is afraid to confront her.

Sometimes older adults harm themselves through self-neglect (e.g., not eating, not going to the doctor for needed care), compulsive hoarding or alcohol or drug abuse. In this book, the focus is on elder abuse perpetrated by others. However, one of the most difficult problems family members face is achieving a balance between respecting an older adult's autonomy and intervening before self-neglect becomes dangerous.

Older adults who show signs of dementia may become abusive as part of the disease process. The object of the abuse may be another adult, for example, a family caregiver, professional caregivers, or other individuals with whom the person interacts. The abuse may take the form of hitting or gripping another person to the extent of causing bruises or creating hazards such as setting furniture on fire. Although abusive behavior by the older adult may be explained by changes in his or her cognitive abilities or triggered by an abusive response by a caregiver, it is still unacceptable.

Abuse comes in many guises, but the net effect is the same. Abuse creates potentially dangerous situations and feelings of worthlessness, and it isolates the older person from people who can help.

Another growing area of concern applies to the vulnerable population of disabled individuals. Some states (including IL) now have mandated reporting laws covering this population.

CHAPTER 9

LICENSING COMPLAINTS

Mental health practitioners are subject to governmental (licensing boards) and legal (professional liability or malpractice) monitoring and regulation. Our profession has become increasingly more regulated and monitored by outside overseers.

The thought of a licensing complaint filed against you can make your knees weak. Allegations of misconduct can be traumatic, expensive, and in some cases career ending. If conduct is criminalized there is also a risk of legal consequences. It is easier to file a complaint than a malpractice action, which requires legal representation. Board complaints can be filed with little paperwork, which may range from one page to five pages. Complaints range from dissatisfaction with services to sexual abuse by therapists. It is not only clients who may file complaints but colleagues as well.

When mental health practitioners procure their licenses, they are making an a priori agreement to abide by the rules of the licensing board in their state and to fully cooperate with a licensing board investigation. Due process protections do not apply. What this means is that there is no right to speedy action. Therefore, I have heard of instances where a practitioner has received notification that the board's findings do not support the allegations and the person has been exonerated. This individual never knew a complaint had been filed against him. The board may notify an individual that a complaint has been filed and the next contact can take months.

It is prudent to understand the scope of the board's authority in your state. Most licensing boards function under administrative law. This area of law governs activities of administrative agencies. Their tasks can include rule making, adjudication on a variety of issues, and enforcement of specific regulatory agendas. If a board feels that an issue such as mental instability compromises your practice, it has the authority to order you to treatment if you wish to maintain your license.

Many board complaints are never investigated. If the board decides that the complaint has no merit or decides not to investigate for any host of reasons, a practitioner may never know that a complaint was ever levied against him or her. Licensing boards have a lot of authority over licensed practitioners. The duty of all boards is to protect the public and regulate the profession. People who report complaints filed against them describe the experience as antagonistic and demeaning. Perhaps this is not true of all states, but it is the trend.

The boards respond to complaints by clients. Initially the board only knows the client's story. Until you respond, the allegations are one sided. The perception of the disciplinary actions taken by a board is dependent on the vantage point from which the process is observed. If a practitioner has a complaint filed against him or her, the board may be perceived as victimizing. As a complainant seeking action by a licensing board, the board may be viewed as vigilant and assuring. Members of the board may perceive themselves as overseers of standards that are set for their profession.

The disciplinary views of the board vary, depending on the membership. Not all boards are composed of solely mental health practitioners. The intent is to make the composition of the board more heterogeneous. Depending on your state the modality of treatment supported by the board might be preferential.

....
Case Example
....

• • • • • • • • • • •

    A psychologist had a complaint filed against her that was evidently substantiated by the board. The board mandated her to receive supervision if she chose to maintain her license and continue to work. She chose a respected colleague to fulfill this role.

    The colleague submitted his résumé to the board for approval as her supervisor. His specialty was a family systems modality. The board was composed, at that time, of individuals who utilized a psychodynamic approach. The prospective supervisor was rejected because the board felt his method was not well grounded.

If a complaint is substantiated, one important area to be familiar with is what is the protocol of appeal. Because a board finding is not a legal resolution, the courts are not usually an option.

There are a host of consequences that may occur, not only those imposed by the board. If you are a provider for an insurance panel, you might be terminated from the panel. Increased insurance premiums may occur. You may be given probationary status in relation to your license or your license suspended for a period of time. Revocation of one's license would be one of the most drastic punishments. Any and all requirements that include questions concerning your practice for future employment must be answered truthfully with a yes. Renewal of state licenses usually requires answering questions in relation to previous board actions. If you decide to practice in another state, that state will ask you questions as to previous board actions. This information is typically available online at the licensure website for any prospective client to see.

The following are some precautionary suggestions. They may not preempt a complaint but will likely place you in a better position to defend yourself if such an action occurs.

Make certain you carry individual malpractice insurance. Many organizations provide policies for their employees. Read the guidelines carefully in both instances. Each insurance policy should include coverage for investigations by the board plus the standard malpractice coverage. The least amount of coverage will likely not cover extensive legal expenses, if needed, because of the lower limit. You might want to consider purchasing the highest coverage available. If you find that your insurance carrier does not provide for protection for board complaints, inquire as to whether you may include it as a rider to your present policy.

If you are dealing with a complicated case, take time out to consult with colleagues about your treatment plan, record keeping, and any other clinical or ethical issues. The outcome of these consultations should be carefully documented in your records including the reasons behind your decision-making. If it isn't written down, it never existed.

If there is ever a board investigation against you, do not dismiss the seriousness because you believe the complaint had nothing to do with your professional judgment. It is important to never take the stance that a complaint filed lacks merit. That decision is up to the board, not to you. Believing that an action will be dismissed if you are provided with the opportunity to explain your chosen actions is foolhardy.

Most boards will inform the practitioner that the process of investigation and decision making is not conducted as if the hearing is taking place in a court of law. The first thing I would recommend would be to hire an attorney and have that person be the conduit with the board. If you receive any requests from the board, from a notice of action letter to a request for records, do not make any information available unless you have consulted with your attorney.

It is not prudent to contact the complainant in an attempt to sort out concerns. It is equally unwise to meet with any board members without legal representation. Attorneys are experts at advising their clients about how to protect themselves from making inadvertent self-incriminatory statements and other unwitting mistakes.

In looking for an attorney be vigilant. You are looking for someone who works with individuals in the mental health profession. Many of these attorneys advertise in the professional journals. You are looking for someone who is experienced working with licensing boards. Many of these attorneys also specialize in assisting mental health practitioners in other legal matters. The knowledge base of the attorney must include familiarity with the mental health laws in your state as well as requirements mandated by the licensing board. Find out how many cases an individual has dealt with in front of which boards. If an attorney tells you they have been practicing in contract law, move on.

BEST PRACTICES

There are many times in practice where we are required to assess difficult clinical situations. Over time as we become more seasoned clinicians, we may integrate different theoretical perspectives to form our own style for assessing and treating clients.

Absence of clearly documented treatment decisions leaves juries free to interpret information as favorable to a plaintiff (suing party). If there is no documented history of what you considered, how you made clinical decisions, the only information available will come from the litigating party. In addition, in a court of law the plaintiff presents its case first. Your mistakes can be misinterpreted to mean that a breach of duty has occurred has been violated, which as we know now, is the first element of a negligence action.

It is critical to make clients aware that early on they may experience a temporary increase in symptoms. The goal, of course, is to decrease the troubling symptoms, but it is unlikely this will occur immediately. Throughout the course of working with a client it is wise to check in with clients as to how they are feeling not only about the precipitating complaint but how the work is going. In medicine the same applies. If a patient contacts a physician for treatment and he or she recommends medications, the side effects of each one will be discussed with the patient

SUICIDE

The national Suicide Prevention Lifeline suggests some suicide risk assessment standards. The subcomponents to examine include suicidal desire, suicidal capability, intent, and what is referred to as a buffer.

If an individual voices suicidal ideation, the desire to kill himself or herself, one of the areas to be assessed should be suicidal capability. A history of suicidal attempts and the potential lethality of those previous attempts are critically important. There is, of course, a dramatic difference between taking ten aspirins and swallowing an entire bottle of a mood stabilizer like lithium. The latter can cause death. This is not to imply that taking fewer pills means that an individual is simply seeking attention, just that the risk is far more immediate for the latter.

The exposure to someone else's suicide increases the risk again. This has been witnessed with adolescents where one person's suicide may lead to a rash of attempts. One of the most important interventions to be considered is hospitalization. This creates a buffer between the thinking and the action. Often, if available, a temporary respite stay might provide the same level of protection. The presence of others provides a decrease in isolation and rumination.

If the client's concerns do not rise to the level of hospitalization, intensifying treatment may be called for: temporarily increasing the frequency of sessions, providing off hours coverage, creating a safety plan, for example.

When an individual feels intense psychological pain and begins to consider a plan with a method, exploration is essential. The individual is likely thinking about stopping the pain. With an intervention that focuses on the future, one can help a person clearly appreciate that the outcome could be death. Hopelessness as part of the psychological ache increases the risk again. An emphasis on the relationship and engagement with the provider may diminish these feelings. Checking in by telephone can be a stabilizing force. Acute onset of symptoms of a serious mental illness, recent mood changes, and psychotic experiences increase the risk, as does intoxication.

You need to keep in mind that if an individual wants to die, sometimes there is very little you can do to intervene. Hospitalized patients where staff are concerned about their suicide risk can be placed on one-to-one supervision for their own protection. Regardless, there are repeated stories of people suiciding at in-patient units.

You do the best you can to try and keep your clients safe. You try to provide a safe environment so people may speak openly about how they are feeling. At times, however, you are helpless. If a seemingly stable client suicides without warning, a court is less likely to be punitive.

Case Example

* * * * * * * * * * * *

I worked with a flight attendant for eight months. She had applied and been accepted into one of the prestigious master of business administration programs. In order for her to attend full time she had to suspend her career. There are benefits for working in the airline industry. Travel is free and hotels provide complimentary room and meals at times. Her desire to remain in one place for a lengthy period of time was an additional driving force.

The decision for acceptance of the offer or deferring to admission was rapidly approaching. She articulated that she had made a decision and had written a letter of resignation that we read together. Without warning she rented a motel room and killed herself with a shotgun. I never knew why or even that she was thinking about suicide.

SELF-INJURIOUS BEHAVIORS

Self-injury is a growing public health concern. It can include scratching or pinching to the point that bleeding occurs or marks are left on the skin, banging or punching one's self to the point of bruising or bleeding, ripping or tearing skin, carving, and burning.

It used to be that self-injurious behaviors were viewed as a suicide attempt that required immediate hospitalization to keep a patient contained. Clinicians who worked with clients who had a history of self-injury were frightened. Many incorrectly assumed these clients fit into the diagnostic grouping referred to as borderline personality, which is incorrect. The goal of treatment often was the creation of a no-harm contract that inevitably resulted in failure.

Individuals who self-injure make mistakes and can suicide inadvertently. Although they usually aren't trying to kill themselves, sometimes they're unable to control the injury and die accidentally.

Consequently, these individuals are high risk to work with. How do clinicians protect themselves from increased liability? It is important to get a baseline understanding of how the clients view their actions. This is made more difficult because self-injury is often secretive and it takes time, in the development of a therapeutic relationship, for a client to disclose the information. It is critical to inquire the meaning of the behaviors for the individual. Sometimes it is a way to express emotional pain from feelings they have no words for; it can be viewed as bloodletting to release toxins they believe are inside their bodies from intense feelings, actions, or thoughts; it can be used to relieve intense emotions; or it may be a way to have control over their bodies when they don't feel control over their lives.

....

Case Example

....

• • • • • • • • • • •

I had a client who had a twenty-year history of cutting herself. She had difficulty with intense emotions and when they peaked she often cut herself to relieve them, like letting the air out of an inflated balloon.

She was consistent in her methodology. She would drive her car to an emergency room parking lot and park out of sight of the hospital entrance, lay a towel over her lap, and proceed to cut herself to the extent she required twelve stitches. She would walk into the emergency room with the bloodied towel wrapped around her arm and announce she had cut herself. Each time the hospital would contact me suggesting immediate admission to a locked psychiatric unit.

These were deep and long cuts. I worried that one might be accidently lethal.

It might be useful to think about a checklist of ideas to assess self-injurious behaviors as a method of risk assessment for clients and risk management for you. Your documentation needs to be meticulous.

The form of self-harm requires specific clarification as well as the intent of the behavior. Once when I was working in a hospital, a patient gouged out his eyeball because he felt it would soothe him from his constant staring. He then announced he was going to begin cutting his chest. This behavior is not self-injury, it is more likely psychotic in nature.

How many wounds per episode? I had a client who carved a pentagram on his chest each time he cut. As time went on, since he cut himself in the same place, the wounds became infected. Nonetheless, he continued. Given the seriousness and frequency of each episode, which had become weekly, I felt that he had crossed a threshold where the cutting threatened his well-being.

It is important to assess the duration of the conduct. Some individuals have brief episodes while others engage in it more often. Others have a ritualistic method of harming themselves and it is savored over a longer period of time.

Which body areas involved also presents risk. There is a difference between a person cutting across a wrist with a razor and making cuts straight down an arm with a knife. Evaluation of the extent of the physical damage should be assessed. Certainly repeatedly cutting a pentagram on one's chest that is left to fester versus a small slice on a person's wrist has different risks.

What instrument is used for the ritual? Razor, kitchen knife, and cigarette produce different levels of injury. It is important to consult with a physician regarding the medical risk of the cutting.

CHILD CUSTODY EVALUATIONS

These types of evaluations are high risk by nature. Custody evaluations whether conducted by court order or independently for divorce is a specialization. The evaluator will most likely get called to court for testimony. The evaluator is required to have knowledge of state statutes and legal precedents, reliable and valid methods identified, as well as the ability to articulate known limitations in data and methods.

From the moment the evaluation is initiated the scope of the evaluation should be described in great detail including limitations of confidentiality if applicable. Meticulous record keeping is a must.

Industrial/organizational and forensic evaluations (e.g. SSI disability) fall in this category as well: highly specialized, high risk for liability, courtroom involvement.

ABANDONMENT AND TERMINATION

Teaching in graduate programs has, over the years, promulgated the idea that despite the nature of a case, the changes or lack of changes that have occurred with the patient or the conduct of a patient, you, as a mental health practitioner, have a duty to treat. This exact view is sometimes reflected in the licensing laws in some states.

This notion is less than accurate since some clinicians may continue with patients that they should be terminating with. Appropriate referrals must be provided.

Distinguishing abandonment from termination can be central to an understanding of what constitutes responsible client care. The definition of abandonment of a professional treatment relationship by a mental health care provider comprises ending the relationship without adequate notice or the patient's consent or providing a competent replacement.

You may have also been taught the myth that a change in a client's financial circumstances or an inability to pay is not grounds to end the treatment. Treatment is a two-way relationship. Contractual obligations should be clearly explained in an informed consent including the obligation on behalf of the patient to pay for services rendered. The informed consent agreement should outline reimbursement issues and how this affects the relationship for continued services. Fiduciary responsibilities are two ways and are more important than just money. It creates a duty and obligation. The relationship is a special kind that requires a client have trust and confidence in the therapist. In creating an environment where a client feels safe to talk about his or her feelings, secrets are a priority

Given the instability of the insurance industry, when coverage changes, you should not be forced to continue treatment. The right to terminate treatment may also happen when, for example, a third-party payer no longer covers professional services. Such a change represents an alteration of the treatment contract agreed on in the original informed consent in relation to money.

If the treater determines that termination is appropriate, consultation with colleagues is imperative as is the documentation of the contact and conversation. Follow-up referrals are mandatory, although the extra step of making sure a contact is made is unnecessary. It is up to the client if they decide to follow-up or not.

A checklist that includes and highlights the following issues in the initial informed consent is judicious.

1. Clarification of the nature and responsibilities of the treatment relationship

2. Limitations of the relationship

③ Financial arrangements

④ Variables that might be considered that lead to the termination of the relationship

Another reason to terminate treatment is the lack of progress. This does not include supportive contacts. The lack of progress suggests unnecessary and ineffective treatment. This is practicing below the standard of care. If a client insists that he or she wants to continue over objections of the psychotherapist, the practitioner is not obligated to continue regardless of the patient's view.

When a clinician feels personally at risk, under threat, simply frightened, or at risk of professional boundary violations for some reason, the provider should discontinue treatment. Mismatch between therapist and patient also requires consideration of termination.

Finally, if a psychotherapist experiences distress, impairment, or illness they should stop practicing. Clients can either be referred to other resources, or a practice may be suspended and someone takes over in the interim.

If your capacity to demonstrate understanding and care for patients is compromised, termination of treatment is unarguably in the best interest of the patient. This is a common blind spot. The clinician feels duty bound to continue seeing the client even when it is no longer in the client's best interest. These cases often end up problematic and may find their way to ethics committees or licensure boards.

Case Example

• • • • • • • • • • •

Ron sought out my services as a psychotherapist. He presented himself as a meek, quiet man. He told me that he was an alcoholic. He would get drunk prior to dinner each evening and incite an argument with his wife. Without alcohol he had difficulty being confrontational. The couple had two children, both girls. Ron dispatched oil trucks for a living. His wife had an all-encompassing corporate executive position. There was a significant power differential between the two and Ron felt over-powered by his wife. Over the previous year their relationship had deteriorated and become acrimonious and distant. They couldn't discuss issues between them calmly or individual responsibilities for child care.

When they had dinner with the children, the arguing was disruptive. Their kids often abruptly left the table, running to their rooms sobbing.

Ron, who was a wonderful father, decided that he wanted to become sober. He gained admission to an outpatient detoxification program. In the morning at the program various groups were held and each afternoon a group of individuals were driven to different AA meetings to find ones they felt comfortable at. For Ron, this was very successful treatment. He completely stopped drinking. He developed a support group at different meetings and had met with a sponsor who he connected with immediately. He also made a schedule for himself for meetings to attend so he could work toward the AA ideology of ninety meetings in ninety days.

As he became more involved in his program of recovery, the household seemed calmer and he began to feel more hopeful. Since his working hours were less than those of his wife, he took over most of the household responsibilities such as cooking meals, laundry, care of the children. His wife rarely came home for dinner with her family. Over time this became a consistent pattern.

Although distressed, he maintained his sobriety. At the end of one workweek, he was laid off, much to his surprise. Now his wife was the sole wage earner in the house and Ron was feeling depressed, alone, and unimportant. He unsuccessfully looked for work. His days were spent walking his girls to school, picking them up, and spending time with them.

However, as his wife increased her time at work, he began to feel abandoned. He and his daughters often ate supper alone. Ron's wife spent less and less time at home.

One morning I received a phone call from him. He said that he had decided to kill himself. He assured me his girls were at school. He was in the basement putting together a noose. While he was on the phone with me, I faxed a "pink paper" to the police (authorizing them to enter the house and take him into custody given that it was an emergency). As I was speaking to him, I heard them arrive and ring the doorbell. Ron ignored it. I suggested to him to let the officers in but he refused. Subsequently, the officer broke the door open, took him into custody, and transferred him to an emergency room for evaluation.

Ron was hospitalized for one week. In my clinical judgment, it was helpful treatment. He was able to think more clearly about his responsibility to his daughters and make contact with his AA supports to talk about what had occurred and schedule meetings and check-ins. While in the hospital he was placed on an antidepressant. He was then discharged and for months seemed to stabilize.

His wife came home one Thursday evening and announced to him that she was not only going to seek divorce but full custody of his children. Later, he was served with papers.

The next morning, Friday, I saw him and heard the news. He was distraught, raging, and talked about abducting his children. He explained that if this wasn't an option he was going to commit suicide.

I inquired whether he thought that a repeat hospitalization might be helpful. He wanted to try to remain safe until Sunday night. I don't make suicide contracts with clients. I believe they are more for my benefit than the patients. We decided together that we would set up a check-in protocol each day to make sure he remained safe. In addition, he agreed to spend the weekend close to his daughters. Ron understood that any deviation from the plan would likely necessitate involuntary hospital admission.

Friday afternoon he called on schedule. I could hear the laughter and splashing in the background. He explained that he had not only taken his daughters but some of their friends to a water park. He said that he felt safe and was buoyed by their joy.

Saturday afternoon he reliably checked in once again. He was at a rolling skating rink with the same group of children. His affect was calmer and more hopeful when we spoke. He assured me that he would be safe and also said that he would not put his children through the loss of their father.

Well, I thought to myself, mission accomplished. On his own, he had found a way to not only stay safe but also increase his hopefulness. We had an appointment scheduled for Sunday evening with a phone call in the morning.

I received a text message that he and his wife were arguing. I replied and reminded him that he had an obligation to call me. He missed our pre-arranged time. I called him on his cell phone and it went directly to voice mail. All texting ceased.

I made a decision to inform the police about his tenuous safety. Just before I faxed the information to the police station and placed a call, his wife texted me that he had hung himself in the basement. He survived only because she went down there and found him hanging and cut him down. I told her to call the police and I did the same.

Ron was taken to the same hospital and this time committed. I felt that this was too close a call. I was going to end our treatment relationship. Why?

1. *Was it because he broke our contract?*
2. *Was he too high risk and therefore placed me at risk?*
3. *Was he not compliant with treatment?*

Although all these reasons might lead in that direction, my main concern was that I had been unable to keep him safe. I believed he needed a higher level of care in an intensive outpatient program (IOP)—quicker and increased access to mental health services that included weekly psychiatric appointments. In addition, I felt that being connected with a clinic he had more immediate access to respite care and would become familiar to providers there. In addition, they had a team of practitioners who visited patients' homes in case of serious concerns about safety or a reported emergency. I believed he needed wrap-around services. Had I continued to work with him, given the recent circumstances, I would have been practicing below what I considered to be the standard of care necessary to assure his safety.

CHAPTER 10

TECHNOLOGY AND CONFIDENTIALITY

The million-dollar question is how do you use technology for therapy? Much to your chagrin it has not been comprehensively answered and may be subject to interpretation.

Social media has taken over the Internet as well as taking up a lot of time in people's lives. Many businesses and organizations have a Facebook page, a Twitter account, a blog, or a LinkedIn profile. Companies use these tools on their websites so that visitors can directly be connected to the company or join in on conversations. You can now have a direct chat with a sales representative of a store to determine size, color, availability, and anticipated fit without ever going to the store.

In the mental health field, technology has certainly opened new doors for client communication among other transmissions of information. Hospitals who use electronic records can now secure them with a code that only permits treatment team members' access to the information. Previously, any person working in the institution had access. Reports can be sent electronically and securely over e-mail.

These changes have not only been rapid but increase the opportunities for different forms of communications. This profession is still trying to answer questions on how to utilize and implement these tools into communications while maintaining boundaries and confidentiality.

Many software packages are available. Products cannot be HIPAA compliant, but as practitioners or institutions, we can be. The idea of being "secure enough" needs careful evaluation. To be secure, the software must meet legal standards and ethical guidelines as well as comport with the HIPAA business associates rule and finally must be useful to the needs of people we work with.

The HIPAA security rule establishes national standards to protect individuals' electronic personal health information that is created, received, used, or maintained by a covered entity. The security rule requires appropriate administrative, physical, and technical safeguards to ensure the confidentiality, integrity, and security of electronic-protected health information.

The privacy rule requires that a covered entity obtain satisfactory assurances from its business associates that each business associate will appropriately safeguard the protected health information it receives or creates on behalf of the covered entity. The satisfactory assurances must be in writing, whether in the form of a contract or other agreement between the covered entity and the business associate.

"A business associate is a person or entity that performs certain functions or activities that involve the use or disclosure of protected health information on behalf of, or provides services to, a covered entity. A member of the covered entity's workforce is not a business associate. A covered health care provider, health plan, or health care clearinghouse can be a business associate of another covered entity." (definition of "business associate" at 45 C.F.R. 160.103).

The HIPAA breach notification rule, (45 C.F.R. §§ 164.400-414), requires HIPAA-covered entities and their business associates to provide notification following a breach of unsecured protected health information.

A breach is an impermissible use or disclosure, under the HIPAA privacy rule, that compromises the security or privacy of protected health information. It is not considered a breach if the entity has demonstrated that there is a low probability that information has been compromised based on a risk assessment of at least the following factors:

- The nature and extent of the information involved, including identifiers and the possibility of identification;
- To whom the disclosure was made, and whether the information was actually acquired or viewed; and
- The possibility of mitigation.

Skype and Facetime, and other video-based forms of therapy, are useful forms of communication, Each is proprietary. Each takes significant precautions to reduce the potential of intercepting communication. Clients who engage in Skype or Facetime therapy must do so with full informed consent of the limitation of privacy and confidentiality.

Cell phone conversations and unsecured e-mail are more vulnerable to privacy breaches. Skype (owned by Microsoft) and Facetime (owned by Apple) are encrypted by default. Nonetheless, if a client gives consent to the use of any of these technologies, informed consent has been obtained.

When the alternative is no treatment at all, it seems obvious to use the accessibility of online options. For example, if a patient lives in an area where few therapists reside or a community is so small that privacy and confidentiality are jeopardized, alternative ways of treatment seem wise. Patients who are bedridden or immobile would benefit from this kind of access. The VA has been at the forefront of using this technology for treating soldiers for PTSD who are still abroad and/or in combat.

Clients can elect to receive unsecured e-mails that contain personal health information from practitioners if they are informed of the risks of e-mail and they still elect to receive the e-mails. It is the client's right to decide to accept the risks of e-mail

Some mediums may be restricted for some clinicians, depending on your state's licensing laws. It is important to review the guidelines of the state you reside in.

Also, as noted earlier, provision of ongoing services such as Skype or Facetime across state lines may raise legal issues if one is not licensed to practice in the state in which the client is located.

Suffice it to say, technological advances have opened up further avenues of vulnerabilities for us as practitioners. Given the lack of clarity on this issue, here are some recommendations:

- Provide a written social media policy and consent form that clients must sign
- Use privacy settings on social media accounts whenever possible
- Check with your state licensing board to stay current on rules and regulations
- Have separate social media accounts for your professional and private use

Most of us utilize copy machines. We can now put a document into the machine for reproduction. If there are many jobs before yours, your document may be entered into a queue and when it is ready an alarm goes off for notification that the job is completed. The data is stored in memory and must be purged to protect confidentiality. Don't accidently leave your documents on the glass. If you no longer need the paper information, shred, shred, shred.

Similarly, fax machines have allowed clinicians to communicate quickly without the burden of time and snail mail. It used to be that when you faxed information you had to wait at the machine until the process was completed.

With advances in technology, fax machines work similarly to copy machines. If you place a document in a machine, without any further action, the machine will attempt to fax the data for the next year. This is particularly important when submitting electronic billing. You might want to consider speed dialing for numbers you repeatedly use. Similarly, data is stored in memory and must be erased. Never send a fax without a cover sheet. Faxes that don't get to their destination go to a place in the sky called faxland!

We routinely use voice mail and answering machines. It is important to make a statement on your voice mail as to the confidentiality parameters. Clients should give their consent for practitioners leaving a message on their voice mail. Texts should be brief such as changing appointment times.

I have a colleague who is a hamburger addict. In one Sunday newspaper section, there was a spread on the ten best hamburger restaurants in the area. I texted her to volunteer to accompany her to her top choice. I received a text back that was not from her. I had texted a client. Don't follow my footsteps.

Many clinicians use computers routinely in their practices. Password protect your entries or use an encryption program. Limit access. Make sure there is a firewall in place. If you back up your data on a hard drive or a CD make sure you follow HIPAA guidelines to protect the information.

Cell phones can be accessed on AM radio or nursery monitors. Many individuals no longer have landlines. Notify clients of the limitations to confidentiality. The same applies to portable phones.

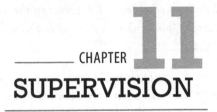

CHAPTER

SUPERVISION

Supervision is a high-risk endeavor for clinicians.

....

Case Example

....

• • • • • • • • • • •

John is a supervisee. A practitioner has been working with him for nine months and John has demonstrated some weaknesses in the application of what he has learned. Although the two parties have tried different ways to help him remediate his performance, it has not been noticeably successful. The supervisor is tasked in training John in the art of clinical practice and also providing him with the opportunity to accumulate hours necessary to meet the requirements for licensure. He wants to take the exam at the end of his training year.

The supervisor has discussed with John his concern with his lagging performance and would like him to seek at minimum six more months of supervision. The supervisor steps forward and even volunteers to assist him.

John comes in one day and announces that he has completed the required paperwork to sit for the licensing examination and he is awaiting confirmation and a date for which he should report to take the exam. It is evident he has not heard about the absence of a recommendation and the persisting problems.

His application is, of course, denied without the recommendation. Subsequently the supervisor receives notification that John has brought a suit against the supervisor for restriction of trade. Restriction of trade is a limitation on the freedom to conduct business. John can't earn a living in this field without a license to practice.

Supervision is a professional practice employing a collaborative working relationship that has both instructive and evaluative components. Goals of supervision include the development of professional competence, monitoring the quality of services provided, protecting the public, ensuring that supervisees meet competency standards in order to advance to the next level or to licensure, and providing a gatekeeping function for entry into the profession. Supervision is not psychotherapy.

I would suggest a written contract between you, as a supervisor, and your supervisee that clearly spells out the responsibilities each undertakes. There are a number of parameters that one might think about in the course of setting up a learning, a teaching, and an evaluating plan.

The purpose and goals of supervision include fulfilling requirements that are necessary for professional competence and identity plus assisting the supervisee in attaining knowledge, conceptualizing, and gaining skills within the individual's field.

The supervisor is tasked with monitoring the supervisee's performance, setting parameters in conjunction with the supervisee of standards of care. Supervisors are required to be knowledgeable about what the supervisee is doing, deal with problems as they affect the supervisee's performance, to create a personal learning and development plan that can be reviewed quarterly.

It is also the supervisor's duty to ensure cultural competence as it relates to individual cases, maintain a collaborative relationship with the goal of promoting the supervisees' learning, to specify the responsibilities and expectations of both parties, and to formulate individual learning goals in conjunction with the supervisee.

Supervisors are tasked with regularly reviewing the progress of the supervisee and the effectiveness of the supervisory relationship and address issues that arise. The responsibility of being the gatekeeper entails assessing supervisees' suitability to enter and remain in the field.

The supervisees' responsibilities include becoming progressively more knowledgeable about diagnoses, interventions, approaches, and techniques; to consult the supervisor or designated contact person in cases of emergency; to follow directives as they apply to their clinical cases; to keep written notes as required by the institution and HIPAA guidelines. Additionally, the supervisees will be required to gain knowledge in ethics, codes, rules, regulations, standards, consent, confidentiality/privacy, and all relevant other legislation.

CHAPTER 12

BALANCING THE RIGHTS OF MINORS AND THEIR PARENTS

Each individual state has its *own* legal guidelines as to the rights of minors seeking help without parental consent. Below is a list of topics that states sometimes address for minors.

Age of Majority

The age of majority defines at what age a minor is treated as an adult. States have laws that define the age. Different states have different ages.

Age of Marriageable Consent

These rules elaborate how old a minor has to be to get married without a parent's consent. These ages vary from state to state so be sure to check your state's laws.

Emancipation of a Minor

Emancipation of minors is a legal mechanism by which a minor is freed from control by his or her parents or guardians, and the parents or guardians are freed from any and all responsibility toward the child. Once declared emancipated, minors have the same rights, privileges, and duties in society as adults. Specific rules vary among the states.

The answer often varies depending on whether parents or the legal system are asked. In family law cases, emancipation of a minor refers to a court process through which a minor can become legally recognized as an independent adult.

All states have laws dealing with specifics defining when and under what conditions children become independent of their parents/guardians.

Summary of Health care Service Options That Can Be Provided to Minors Without Parental Consent

Items that need to be addressed for treatment of a minor without parental consent are the following:

(1) Minor consent sufficient for confidential care

(2) Parent/Guardian consent required

(3) Parent/Guardian notification required

Services That May Be Requested by a Minor

- Emergency medical services
- Nonemergency medical services
- Immunizations
- Sexually transmitted disease testing/treatment (including HIV)
- Birth control services, contraception
- Abortion services
- Prenatal care services
- Care of children born to a minor
- Inpatient mental health care
- Outpatient mental health care
- Inpatient substance abuse treatment
- Outpatient substance abuse treatment
- Privacy and confidentiality of mental health records
- Dental treatment

Best Interests of the Child

Across all states in divorce or custody cases, all decisions are made by a court of law where the best interests of the child are the guiding principles. Below are a number of considerations that a court might take into consideration. States vary on these variables. It is up to the discretion of each court to use all, some, or none of them.

- Maintain a loving, stable relationship with the children
- Provide for the children's basic needs, such as feeding, clothing, physical health, grooming, health care, day care, etc.

- Be involved with the educational needs of the children
- Exercise sound judgment
- Financially support the children
- Domestic violence in the home
- Substance abuse of the parents

AUTHOR BIOGRAPHY

 **SUSAN J. LEWIS PH.D., J.D.**, is a mental health professional with a unique combination as a licensed psychologist, forensic psychologist, and attorney. For more than 25 years, Dr. Lewis has maintained a private clinical practice in Massachusetts, working with couples, families, individuals, and groups. She is a national speaker and has taught continuing education courses on *Law and Ethics in Mental Health* and the *DSM-5*. She has served as a consultant to various organizations including clinics, hospitals, and universities. Dr. Lewis regularly works with attorneys on controversial issues such as dangerousness, competence to stand trial, criminal responsibility evaluations, and civil and criminal commitment. She has been adjudicated as an expert in almost all of the district and superior courts in Massachusetts.

Dr. Lewis has served in leadership roles as a clinical director and program manager, as well as a supervisor for psychiatry residents and post-doctoral psychology interns. She has taught courses at Harvard's Extension School and Northeastern University on *The Psychology of Criminal Behavior*. Recently Dr. Lewis relocated from Massachusetts to Colorado and is involved in similar work as in Massachusetts, although it is at a higher altitude!

References

Barnett, J. E. (2008). The ethical practice of psychotherapy: easily within our reach. *Journal of clinical psychology, 64*(5), 569–575.

Davis, D.D. & Younggren, J. N. (2009) Ethical competence in psychotherapy termination. *Professional Psychology: Research and Practice, 40*(6), 572–578.

Fisher, M.A. (2008) Protecting confidentiality rights: The need for an ethical practice model *American Psychologist, 63*(1), 1–13.

Grand, D. (2013). Brainspotting: The revolutionary new therapy for rapid and effective change. Boulder, CO: Sounds True.

Haney C., Banks C., Zimbardo, P. (1973) Interpersonal dynamics in a simulated prison. International journal of criminology and penology. 1, 69–97.

Jennings, F. L. & J. R. Hays. (2011) How are treating psychologists to respond to requests for court testimony? *Open Access Journal of Forensic Psychology* (3) 20–30.

Linehan MM. (1993) Cognitive-Behavioral Treatment of Borderline Personality Disorder. New York, NY: Guilford Press.

Milgram, S. (1963). Behavioral study of obedience. Journal of abnormal and social psychology, 67, 371.

Pope, K., Vasquez, M. J. T. (2016) Ethics in Psychotherapy and Counseling: A Practical Guide (5th edition), Wiley & Sons: New Jersey.

Shapiro, F. (1989). Eye movement desensitization: A new treatment for post-traumatic stress disorder. Journal of Behavior Therapy and Experimental Psychiatry, 20, 211–217.

Simon, S. & Schuman, D.W. (2009) Therapeutic Risk Management of Clinical-Legal Dilemmas: Should It Be a Core Competency? *J Am Acad Psychiatry Law* 37:2:155–161.

Smith, J. A., Pomerantz, A. M., Pettibone, J. C., & Segrist, D. J. (2012). When does a professional relationship with a psychologist begin? An empirical investigation. *Ethics & Behavior, 22*(3), 208–217.

Thomas, J.T. (2007) Informed consent through contracting for supervision: minimizing risks, enhancing benefits. *Professional Psychology: Research and Practice 38*(3) 221–231.

Thomas, J.T. (2007) Informed consent through contracting for supervision: minimizing risks, enhancing benefits. *Professional Psychology: Research and Practice 38*(3) 221–231.

Younggren, J. N., Fisher, M. A., Foote, W. E., & Hjelt, S. E. (2011). A legal and ethical review of patient responsibilities and psychotherapist duties. *Professional Psychology: Research and Practice, 42*(2), 160–168.

Younggren, J. N., & Gottlieb, M. C. (2008). Termination and abandonment: History, risk, and risk management. *Professional Psychology: Research and Practice, 39*(5), 498.

Zur, O. (2007). *Boundaries in Psychotherapy: Ethical and Clinical Explorations.* American Psychological Association.